Common Japanese Collocations

Common Japanese Collocations

A Learner's Guide to Frequent Word Pairings

Kakuko Shoji
Supervising Editor

KODANSHA INTERNATIONAL
Tokyo • New York • London

This book was produced by Nihon IR Inc., also known as JIRCO.

Distributed in the United States by Kodansha America, LLC, and in the United Kingdom and continental Europe by Kodansha Europe Ltd. Published by Kodansha International Ltd., 17-14 Otowa 1-chome, Bunkyo-ku, Tokyo 112-8652.

First edition, 2010
18 17 16 15 14 13 12 11 10   10 9 8 7 6 5 4 3 2 1

Library of Congress Cataloging-in-Publication Data

Common Japanese collocations : a learner's guide to frequent word pairings / supervising editor: Kakuko Shoji.
      p. cm.
  ISBN 978-4-7700-3123-5
1. Japanese language—Textbooks for foreign speakers—English. 2. Japanese language—Grammar. 3. Japanese language—Usage. I. Shoji, Kakuko.
  PL539.5.E5C66 2010
  495.6'82421—dc22

                                          2010009526

www.kodansha-intl.com

CONTENTS

PREFACE

This book is intended as a guide to Japanese usage. It has been designed for learners of all levels, with the hope that they will discover new ways of saying things.

Oftentimes, even in English, we are unsure about the meanings of certain words, and sometimes we misuse the most ordinary of expressions. Naturally, this happens with much more frequency when we are learning a foreign language. This book presents more than 3,200 collocations, or word combinations, to help students improve the naturalness of their spoken Japanese. Included are phrases the Japanese use all the time in day-to-day life, as well as a large number of idiomatic phrases and special expressions that reflect Japanese thought and culture. To the extent possible, word combinations have been selected based on frequency of use, with phrases revealing emotional or psychological states forming the heart of the book. There are also plenty of quotidian noun-and-verb or noun-and-adjective combinations that are simply useful to know.

To make the collocations easier to study, we have arranged them thematically into chapters rather than listing them alphabetically or in Japanese a-i-u-e-o order. Since it is the noun that is usually known, the collocations are listed under noun headwords. Within each entry, we try to show the full range of usage, and when a particular word combination is hard to understand on its own, we have given an example sentence to demonstrate its usage. For all kanji characters or compounds, we have supplied readings in the form of *furigana*.

This book is the result of painstaking efforts by a number of people, namely Michael Staley at Kodansha International, who directed the project, and Tamiko Fujiwara and her team at Nihon IR Inc., who selected the collocations and translated them into English. To these individuals and to everyone who contributed, I would like to express my sincere thanks.

Kakuko Shoji
Spring 2010

HOME

Body & Hygiene

（お）風呂・湯船
bath, bathtub

風呂に（お）湯を入れる run a hot bath; fill up the bath-tub with hot water

ホテルの部屋に戻ると、すぐにお風呂にお湯を入れた。As soon as I got back to my hotel room, I ran a hot bath.

風呂の（お）湯を落とす pull the plug out of the bathtub (and drain the water)

風呂を沸かす prepare the bath

帰ったらすぐにお風呂に入りたいから、お風呂を沸かしておいてね。I want to take a bath right after I get home, so will you prepare it for me?

風呂が沸いている the bath is ready

風呂を（水で）うめる make the bath water less hot (by adding cold water)

風呂に入る take a bath

風呂／湯船につかる soak in a bathtub

こんな寒い日は、熱いお風呂にゆっくりつかりたい。On a cold day like this, I feel like soaking in a nice hot bath.

風呂から上がる get out of the bath

一風呂浴びる take a bath

一風呂浴びてビールにしよう。I think I'll take a bath and then have some beer.

（お）湯・水
hot water, water

風呂で汗を流す wash off one's sweat in the bath

お湯を冷ます let (hot) water cool down

お湯が冷める hot water cools down

お湯をうめる add cold water (to the bath) to lower the

temperature

お湯がぬるい the water is lukewarm

顔を洗う wash one's face

朝起きると、顔を洗うより先に猫にえさをやります。
I feed my cats first thing in the morning, even before washing my face.

顔を（タオル／手拭いで）拭く dry one's face (with a towel)

顔（のうぶ毛）を剃る shave (the fuzz on) one's face

週に１度、顔のうぶ毛を剃ります。I shave (the fuzz on) my face once a week.

顔
（体・頭・手・足）
face, body, head,
hand, foot, etc.

髪（の毛）
hair

髪を洗う wash one's hair

髪を乾かす dry one's hair

ゆうべ髪をよく乾かさずに寝たので、ひどい寝ぐせがついてしまった。My hair got really messy because I went to bed without drying it last night.

髪を（くしで）とかす／髪にブラシをかける comb/brush one's hair

１時間も寝坊してあわてて家を出たので、髪をとかすひまもなかった。I overslept for an hour and rushed out of the house, so I didn't have time to brush my hair.

髪をブローする blow-dry one's hair

美容院でやってくれるように、うまく髪をブローすることができない。I can't blow-dry my hair as well as they do at my hairdresser.

髪の手入れをする take care of one's hair

シャワー
shower

シャワーを浴びる take a shower

朝はいつもシャワーを浴びてはじめて目が覚める。
I'm not really awake in the morning until I take a shower.

シャワーを使う use a shower

昨日の夜は断水でシャワーを使えなかった。I couldn't use the shower since the water supply was cut off last night.

シャンプー
shampoo

シャンプーする shampoo one's hair

美容院でシャンプーしてもらうのが好きです。I like

having my hair shampooed at a beauty salon.

シャンプーを使う use shampoo

どの銘柄のシャンプーを使っていますか？ Which brand of shampoo do you use?

シャンプーで洗う wash with shampoo

シャンプーを洗い流す rinse one's hair

シャンプーを切らす run out of shampoo

シャンプーを切らしてしまったんだけど、借りてもいい？ Can I use your shampoo? I've run out ...

シャンプーを変える change (the brand of) shampoo

せっけん
soap

せっけんを使う use soap

油の汚れは、せっけんを使わないとなかなか落ちない。You can hardly get rid of the grease without soap.

せっけんで／せっけんをつけて洗う wash with soap

インフルエンザの予防には、手をよくせっけんで洗うことが重要だ。It's important to wash your hands well in order to prevent catching the flu.

せっけんを泡立てる lather up soap

トイレ・
お手洗い・便所
toilet, bathroom

トイレ／お手洗いに行く go to the bathroom

トイレに行きたくなってきた。I need/have to go to the bathroom.

トイレに入る go to the bathroom

トイレを借りる／使わせてもらう use the bathroom

散歩の途中、コンビニに寄ってトイレを借りた。During the walk, I stopped by at a convenience store and used the bathroom.

トイレがふさがっている［空いている］the bathroom is occupied [not occupied]

休憩時間にトイレに行ったが、すべてのトイレがふさがっていた。I went to the restroom during the intermission, but all the toilets were occupied.

便所と書いてある the sign says "benjo"

『便所』と書いてあるでしょう。あそこがトイレです。Do you see the sign that says "benjo"? That's the

歯
teeth

bathroom.

歯を磨く brush one's teeth

私は毎食後に歯を磨きます。 I brush my teeth after every meal.

歯(と歯)の間をきれいにする brush between one's teeth

歯(と歯)の間をフロスする floss; clean between one's teeth with dental floss

歯(と歯の間)に(ものが)挟まる something gets stuck between one's teeth

肌
skin

肌が乾燥する get dry skin; one's skin dries

冬になると肌が乾燥して、かゆくなることがある。 In winter my skin gets dry and sometimes it causes itchiness.

肌が荒れる get rough skin; one's skin gets rough

肌の手入れをする take care of one's skin

彼女はお風呂上がりに、肌の手入れを欠かしません。 She never fails to take good care of her skin after taking a bath.

肌を焼く get suntanned; tan oneself

最近は、夏でも肌を焼きたくないという人が、多くなってきている。 Fewer people are willing to get suntanned in summer these days.

肌が(日焼けで)赤くなる one's skin gets red (because of sunburn)

肌がひりひりする one's skin smarts (from sunburn)

(うるし・化粧品で)肌がかぶれる get a rash (caused by exposure to lacquer/cosmetics); break out

肌がしっとりする one's skin is soft (and moist)

髭
mustache, beard

髭を剃る shave

髭を剃っていたら、誤って少し切ってしまった。 I accidentally cut myself a little while I was shaving.

髭を剃り落とす shave off one's mustache/beard

彼は髭を剃り落としていて、まるで別人のようだった。 He had shaved off his beard and looked totally different.

髭をたくわえる have a mustache/beard

その国では、ほとんどの成人男性は髭をたくわえている。Almost all adult men have a mustache or beard in that country.

髭を伸ばす grow a mustache/beard

生まれて初めて髭を伸ばしてみることにした。I've decided to grow a mustache for the first time in my life.

髭が伸びる one's beard grows

解放されたとき、人質は髭が伸びて疲れ切った様子だった。The hostage was unshaven and looked exhausted when released.

髭を生やす grow a mustache/beard

無精髭が生えている be unshaven

髭が濃くなる one's beard thickens

髭を整える trim one's mustache/beard

Makeup

**アイシャドウ
eye shadow**

アイシャドウをつける apply eye shadow

アイシャドウを塗る put on eye shadow

アイシャドウをのせる put on eye shadow

まぶた全体に、明るい色のアイシャドウをのせます。Put on the highlighter eye shadow across the eyelid.

アイシャドウをぼかす smudge eye shadow

指で濃い色のアイシャドウをぼかして、なじませます。Smudge the dark eye shadow with your finger and blend well.

**アイライン
eyeliner**

アイラインを入れる apply eyeliner

うちの犬は、まるでアイラインを入れたかのような目をしている。My dog's eyes look as if someone has applied eyeliner to them.

アイラインを引く apply eyeliner

アイラインがいつもうまく引けない。I can never apply eyeliner very well.

口紅 (くちべに)
lipstick

アイラインを描 (か) く apply eyeliner

アイラインがにじむ eyeliner runs

口紅 (くちべに) をつける put on lipstick

鏡 (かがみ) を見ないで口紅 (くちべに) をつけたら、唇 (くちびる) からはみ出 (だ) してい
た。I put on lipstick without looking in the mirror
and it went over my lip line.

口紅 (くちべに) をつけている be wearing lipstick

口紅 (くちべに) を塗 (ぬ) る put on lipstick

口紅 (くちべに) を落とす remove lipstick

(シャツに) 口紅 (くちべに) がつく／ついている (a shirt) gets/is
stained with lipstick

着替 (きが) えたとき、白 (しろ) いシャツに口紅 (くちべに) がついてしまった。
My white shirt got stained with lipstick when I
changed clothes.

口紅 (くちべに) が落ちる one's lipstick wears off

食事 (しょくじ) をすると、どうしても口紅 (くちべに) が落ちてしまう。
Lipstick inevitably wears off after having a meal.

口紅 (くちべに) がはげる one's lipstick wears off

口紅 (くちべに) を (塗 (ぬ) り／つけ) 直 (なお) す touch up one's lipstick

レストランのテーブルに着いたまま、口紅 (くちべに) を塗 (ぬ) り直 (なお)
すのは見苦 (みぐる) しい。It's unbecoming to touch up your
lipstick at the table in a restaurant.

口紅 (くちべに) を拭 (ふ) き取 (と) る wipe off one's lipstick

化粧 (けしょう)・メーク
makeup

化粧 (けしょう) (を) する make (oneself) up; put on one's makeup;
wear makeup

ふだんは、ほとんど化粧 (けしょう) をしません。Usually I don't
wear makeup.

薄化粧 (うすげしょう) をする put on light makeup

化粧 (けしょう) が濃 (こ) い one's makeup is heavy/thick; wear thick
makeup

そのタレントは、ちょっと化粧 (けしょう) が濃すぎる。That TV
personality wears a bit too much makeup.

化粧 (けしょう) が上手 (じょうず) ［下手 (へた)］だ be good [poor] at applying makeup

化粧 (けしょう) を落 (お) とす remove/take off one's makeup

家に帰ると、化粧も落とさずにそのまま寝てしまった。
When I got home, I went straight to bed without even taking off my makeup.

化粧を直す fix/touch up one's makeup

化粧ののりがよい one's makeup holds well
ゆうべはよく寝たせいか、今日は化粧ののりがいい。
My makeup held well, maybe because I had a good sleep last night.

化粧ののりが悪い one's makeup doesn't hold well
疲れているときは、化粧ののりが悪い。When you are tired, makeup doesn't hold very well.

ほお紅
rouge, blush

ほお紅をつける／塗る rouge one's cheeks; put on blush
ほお紅をつけるときは、プロ仕様の大きなブラシを使うといい。When applying the blush, it's better to use a big professional brush.

ほお紅をさす lightly rouge one's cheeks

ほお紅を落とす remove blush

マスカラ
mascara

マスカラをつける put on mascara; apply mascara

マスカラをつけている wear mascara
彼女は着ている服に合わせて、ブルーのマスカラをつけていた。She was wearing blue mascara to match her outfit.

マスカラを塗る put on mascara

マスカラを落とす remove mascara
マスカラを落とすのに、専用のリムーバーを使っています。I use a special remover to take off mascara.

マスカラがにじむ one's mascara smudges around one's eyes
鏡を見ると、マスカラがにじんでパンダのようになっていた。When I looked in the mirror, I found that my mascara had smudged around my eyes like a panda.

マスカラがダマになる get clumpy mascara build-up
マスカラがダマになるのを防ぐには、どうすればいいですか？ How can I avoid getting clumpy mascara build-up?

Clothing & Accessories

上着・コート
jacket, coat

上着を着る put on one's jacket
上着を脱ぐ take off one's jacket
レストランで上着を脱いで、そのまま置いてきてしまった。I took off my jacket in the restaurant and left it there by accident.
上着を羽織る put one's jacket on one's shoulders
上着をハンガーにかける put one's jacket on a hanger
上着を脱ぎ捨てる cast/throw off one's jacket
上着を預ける check one's coat
クロークで上着を預けましょう。Let's check our coats at the cloakroom.

傘
umbrella

傘をさす open an umbrella
彼は大雨の中を傘もささずに歩いていた。He was walking in the heavy rain without an umbrella.
傘を開く［閉じる／たたむ］open [close] an umbrella
傘をすぼめる close an umbrella halfway; have an umbrella half closed
傘を持って行く bring an umbrella
天気予報では夕方から雨らしいから、傘を持って行きなさい。The weather report says it will rain this evening, so take your umbrella with you.
傘を持ち歩く carry an umbrella
傘を置き忘れる leave an umbrella behind
また電車に傘を置き忘れてしまった。I left my umbrella in the train again.
傘をなくす lose one's umbrella
私はすぐ傘をなくすから、安いビニール傘で十分だ。I keep losing my umbrellas, so a cheap plastic one is good enough for me.
傘をさしかける share one's umbrella
可愛い女の子が傘をさしかけてくれた。A pretty girl shared her umbrella with me.
傘に入れてもらう come under someone else's umbrella

彼女は傘を持っていなかったので、駅まで傘に入れてあげた。She didn't have her umbrella with her, so we shared mine to the station.

傘を間違える take the wrong umbrella

(濡れた)傘を干す／乾かす dry an umbrella

傘が(強風で)お猪口になる an umbrella is blown inside out (by a strong wind)

かばん・バッグ
bag

かばんを持つ have a bag (in one's hand)

彼は大きなかばんを持っていたので、どこか旅行に行ったのかもしれない。He might have gone on a trip since he had a big bag with him.

かばんを(ホテル／タクシーに)忘れ(てく)る leave one's bag behind (in the hotel/taxi)

かばんから取り出す take ... out of one's bag

彼はかばんから、分厚い本を取り出した。He took a thick book out of his bag.

かばんに入れる put ... in one's bag

かばんにしまう put ... in one's bag

大事な書類なので、なくさないようにすぐにかばんにしまった。I put those important papers in my bag right away so that I wouldn't lose them.

かばんをなくす lose one's bag

かばんを盗まれる have one's bag stolen

かばんを置き忘れる leave one's bag behind

電車の網棚に、かばんを置き忘れた。I left my bag on a rack in the train.

靴下・靴
socks, shoes

靴下を履く put on one's socks

寒がりなので、朝起きたらすぐに靴下を履きます。I'm very sensitive to the cold, so I put on my socks first thing in the morning.

靴下を脱ぐ take off one's socks

靴下を脱いだら、脱ぎっぱなしにしないで洗濯機に入れてください。When you take off your socks, don't just leave them anywhere—put them in the washer.

靴下を履き替える change one's socks

靴のひもを結ぶ lace up one's shoes; tie one's shoelaces

息子はまだ自分で靴のひもが結べない。My son can't tie his shoelaces by himself.

靴のひもをほどく unlace one's shoes; untie one's shoelaces

靴のひもがほどけている one's shoelaces are undone

靴を磨く polish one's shoes

この間、自動で靴を磨く機械を見かけました。The other day I saw a machine that automatically polishes your shoes.

靴(のサイズ)が合わない the shoes don't fit

ジーンズ・スカート・ズボン
jeans, skirt, pants

ズボンをはく put on pants

ズボンをはいている wear pants

ふだんはいつもズボンで、めったにスカートははきません。I always wear pants and seldom wear a skirt.

ズボンを脱ぐ take off one's pants

ズボンをはき替える change one's pants

ズボンにアイロンをかける／ズボンをプレスする iron/press trousers

パーティーに着ていくスーツのズボンに、アイロンをかけた。I ironed the trousers of the suit I am going to wear to the party.

ズボンに折り目をつける put a crease in one's trousers; crease one's trousers

ズボン(のすそ)をまくり上げる roll up the cuffs of one's pants

下着
underwear

下着をつける put on underwear

公衆浴場では、絶対に下着をつけたまま入浴してはいけません。Never go into a public bath with your underwear on.

下着をとる take off one's underwear

下着を替える change one's underwear

シャツ・セーター
shirt, sweater

シャツを着る put on a shirt

シャツを脱ぐ take off one's shirt

シャツを着替える change shirts

セーターを後ろ前に着る a sweater is on backwards

セーターを後ろ前に着ていたことに、1日中気づか

なかった。I didn't notice that my sweater was on

backwards all day.

シャツを裏返しに着る wear a shirt inside out

シャツにアイロンをかける iron/press a shirt

シャツのすそを出す wear one's shirt untucked

最近、シャツのすそを出すのが、はやっているみた

い。Recently it seems to be fashionable to wear shirts

untucked.

すそ
hem

すそを上げる have the hem taken up; take up (the skirt)

その店ではジーンズのすそを上げてもらうのに、3 0

分もかからない。It takes less than half an hour to have

your jeans hemmed up at that shop.

すそを出す have the hem let down

すそを引きずる trail ... on the ground

フラメンコダンサーは、すそを引きずるような衣装

をつけて踊っていた。The flamenco dancer was danc-

ing in a costume that trailed on the floor.

すそをまくる／まくり上げる roll up the cuffs (of one's

pants)

ズボンのすそをまくり上げて、波打ち際を歩いた。I

rolled up the cuffs of my pants and waded along the

shore.

すそを折り返す roll up (one's trousers); fold up the bot-

tom of ...

(着物の)すそを持つ hold the hem of one's kimono

そで
sleeve

そでが長い［短い］be long-sleeved [short-sleeved]

このジャケット、サイズはぴったりだけど、ちょっ

とそでが短いみたい。This jacket fits me just right,

except the sleeves are a little too short.

そでをまくる／まくり上げる roll up one's sleeves

腕相撲をしようと言うと、彼は早速そでをまくり

上げて応じた。When I challenged him to arm wres-

tling, he readily accepted and rolled up his sleeve.

そでを引っ張る pull ... by the sleeve

そでを通す put ... on

初めてそのユニフォームにそでを通したときの喜びは、忘れられない。I'll never forget how happy I was when I put on the uniform for the first time.

手袋
gloves

手袋をする put on one's gloves

彼女は洗い物をするとき、必ずゴム手袋をしている。She always puts on her rubber gloves when doing the dishes.

手袋をはめる put on gloves

手袋をはずす take off one's gloves

手袋を取る take off one's gloves

手袋をはめたままでいる keep one's gloves on

手袋をはめたままで握手をするのは、失礼ですよ。It's rude to shake hands with your gloves on.

ネクタイ
tie

ネクタイを締める／する wear/put on a tie

ネクタイをするのは年に数回だ。I wear a tie only a couple of times a year.

クライアントとの打ち合わせのときは、ネクタイを締めることになっている。We are supposed to wear a tie when having a meeting with our clients.

ネクタイを直す fix one's tie

ネクタイをゆるめる loosen one's tie

ネクタイを取る take off one's tie

パジャマ・
寝間着
pajamas

パジャマを着る put on one's pajamas

パジャマに着替える change into one's pajamas

パジャマを脱ぐ take off one's pajamas

ファスナー
zipper

ファスナーを上げる／締める zip up; zip ... shut

背中のファスナーが、自分で上げられない。I can't pull up the zipper on my back by myself.

ファスナーを下ろす／開ける unzip; zip ... open

ファスナーが壊れる a zipper breaks

かばんのファスナーが壊れて閉まらなくなった。The zipper on my bag broke and doesn't zip shut anymore.

ファスナーがかむ a zipper gets stuck

ファスナー(の金具)が外れる the slider of a zipper comes off

ファスナーを閉め忘れる forget to zip (one's pants, etc.)

服
clothes

服を着る put on clothes

彼女はいつも自分によく似合う服を着ている。 She always wears clothes that look really good on her.

服を脱ぐ take off one's clothes

服を着替える change one's clothes

服を着替えるのに、こちらの部屋を使ってください。 Please use this room for changing clothes.

服にブラシをかける brush off one's clothes

服を選ぶ choose which clothes to wear

友達の結婚式に着ていく服を選ぶのに、付き合ってもらえますか？ Would you help me choose which clothes to wear to my friend's wedding?

服(のサイズ)が合わない clothes don't fit someone

服が汚れる one's clothes get dirty

ベルト
belt

ベルトをする put on a belt

このベルトをしていると、必ず空港の金属探知機に引っかかってしまう。 I can never walk through the metal detector at an airport with this belt on.

ベルトを締める put on a belt

ベルトをつける put on a belt

ベルトをきつくする tighten one's belt

ベルトをゆるめる loosen one's belt

食べ放題の店で食べ過ぎて苦しくなり、ベルトをゆるめた。 I was so full after eating too much at an all-you-can-eat restaurant that I loosened my belt.

ベルトを外す take off one's belt

帽子
hat, cap

帽子をかぶる put on a hat/cap

その町の男性は、みな独特の帽子をかぶっていた。 All the men in the city wore a characteristic cap.

帽子を目深にかぶる wear a hat low over one's eyes

帽子をとる take off one's hat

挨拶するときには、帽子をとるのがエチケットだ。It is good manners to take off your hat when greeting somebody.

帽子を脱ぐ take off one's hat

女性は室内でも帽子を脱ぐ必要はない。Women don't need to take their hats off even indoors.

（風で飛ばないように）帽子を押さえる hold one's hat (so it won't be blown off)

ボタン
button

ボタンを留める do up the buttons; button (up)

利き手をけがしたので、ボタンを留めるのが大変です。It's difficult to do up the buttons because I injured my dominant hand.

ボタンをかける do up the buttons

ボタンをかけ違える button up the wrong way

今朝は大急ぎで着替えたので、ボタンをかけ違えていた。I got dressed in such a hurry this morning that I buttoned up the wrong way.

ボタンをはずす undo the buttons; unbutton

ボタンがはずれている a button is undone

ボタンが取れる a button comes off

満員電車でもみくちゃにされて、コートのボタンが取れそうになった。One of my coat buttons was about to come off after I was jostled in a packed train.

ボタンをつける sew a button on ...

シャツにボタンをつけたいのですが、裁縫道具を貸してもらえませんか？ Could I borrow your sewing kit? I need to sew a button on my shirt ...

眼鏡
glasses

眼鏡をかける／する put on one's glasses

眼鏡をかけている wear glasses

前から2列目の、眼鏡をかけている人が私の姉です。The person wearing glasses in the second row from the front is my sister.

眼鏡をはずす／取る take off one's glasses

眼鏡を取ると1メートル先の人の顔も、よくわからない。Without my glasses, I can't even recognize someone just a meter away

眼鏡が曇る one's glasses fog up

ラーメンを食べるとき、いつも眼鏡が曇るのがうっとうしい。Every time I eat ramen, my glasses fog up, which is annoying.

眼鏡を拭く clean/wipe one's glasses

眼鏡が壊れる one's glasses break

眼鏡のレンズがはずれる a lens comes off its frame

眼鏡の度を変える change the thickness of a lens

**指輪
ring**

指輪をする wear a ring

彼女は左手の薬指に指輪をしていた。She was wearing a ring on her left ring finger.

指輪をはめる put on a ring

指輪をつける put on a ring

結婚していますが、ふだんは指輪をつけていません。I'm married but I usually don't wear my wedding ring.

指輪をはずす take off a ring

指輪をあつらえる order a ring

指輪を贈る give a ring

Housework

**洗い物
things to wash,
the dishes,
laundry**

洗い物をする do the dishes

うちでは、料理を作るのと洗い物をするのを、交代でやっています。We take turns preparing food and doing the dishes.

洗い物がたまっている have a lot of dishes/clothes to wash

シンクに洗い物がたまっている状況が嫌なので、食器はすぐ洗う。I do the dishes right away because I hate having the sink filled with dirty dishes.

洗い物を手伝う help with the dishes

洗い物をすませる finish (doing) the dishes

ゴミ
garbage, trash

ゴミを出す take out the garbage
毎朝ゴミを出すのは、私の役目だ。It's my job to take out the garbage every morning.

ゴミを分別する sort garbage
きちんとゴミを分別するように、大家さんから注意された。I was warned by the landlord to sort my garbage.

ゴミを捨てる dump trash

ゴミを拾う pick up trash

ゴミを持ち帰る take one's trash home
自分で出したゴミは、必ず持ち帰ってください。Make sure that you take your own trash home.

ゴミがたまる trash collects/accumulates

ゴミが出る produce garbage
この料理は大根の皮まで使うので、ゴミが出ません。This dish even uses the skin of the daikon radish, so there is no waste.

ゴミになる become trash; be thrown away as trash

ゴミを集める／収集する collect/pick up garbage

ゴミを焼却する incinerate garbage

しみ
stain

しみを取る remove a stain

しみを抜く remove a stain

しみをつける make a stain
ワインをこぼして、テーブルクロスに思いっきりしみをつけてしまった。I accidentally spilled wine and made a big stain on the tablecloth.

しみが落ちる a stain comes off
このクリーナーを使うと、簡単にしみが落ちます。Stains come off easily with this cleaner.

しみになる get stained
しみになるといけないから、すぐに洗ったほうがいい。You should wash it right away, or it may get stained.

洗濯
washing

洗濯(を)する wash; do the washing/laundry
上の階の住人は、よく夜遅くに洗濯をする。The per-

son living above me often does their laundry late at night.

洗濯がきく／洗濯できる　be washable

このジャケットは、家で洗濯できますか？ Is this jacket washable?

洗濯に出す　send ... to the laundry

洗濯物
laundry

洗濯物を干す　hang the laundry (out) to dry

やっと晴れたので、洗濯物を外に干すことができる。

It finally cleared up, and now I can hang the laundry out to dry.

洗濯物を取り込む　bring in the washing

夕方からは雨みたいだから、昼すぎには洗濯物を取り込んでおいてね。They say it will rain in the evening, so bring in the washing in the afternoon.

洗濯物をたたむ　fold up the clean clothes

洗濯物がたまる　the laundry piles up

雨降りの日が続いたので、洗濯物がたまっています。I have lots of clothes to wash after the wet spell.

洗濯物が(雨で)濡れる　the laundry gets wet (in the rain)

洗濯物が乾く　the laundry dries

ぞうきん
cleaning rag

ぞうきんを(固く)絞る　wring out a cleaning rag (well)

ぞうきんを固く絞って、たたみを拭いた。I wrung out the cleaning rag well and wiped the tatami mats.

ぞうきんで(床を)拭く　wipe/clean (the floor) with a cleaning rag

ぞうきんを洗う　wash a cleaning rag

ぞうきんを干す　hang a cleaning rag to dry

(床に)ぞうきんをかける／ぞうきんがけをする　wipe the floor with a cleaning rag

毎朝修行僧たちが、寺中のぞうきんがけをする。

Every morning, Buddhist trainee monks wipe the entire floor of the temple with cleaning rags.

(乾いた)ぞうきんで床を磨く　polish the floor with a (dry) cleaning rag

（ドライ） クリーニング **(dry) cleaning**	クリーニングする have ... dry-cleaned クリーニングに出す send ... to the (dry) cleaners 　冬物のコートやジャケットを、全部まとめてクリーニングに出した。I sent all the winter coats and jackets to the dry cleaners. クリーニングから戻ってくる come back from the cleaners 　そのワンピースは、まだクリーニングから戻ってきていません。The dress hasn't come back from the cleaners.
ひも **cord, string**	ひもを結ぶ tie a string ひもをほどく untie a string ひもを通す run a string through ... ひもで縛る／くくる tie with a string 　新聞をいくつかの束にまとめて、ひもで縛った。I made several bundles of newspapers and tied them with a string. ひもをかける tie with a string
ほうき **broom**	ほうきで掃く sweep with a broom ほうきで掃除する clean with a broom ほうきで掃き集める sweep ... up with a broom 　地元のボランティアたちが、ほうきで落ち葉を掃き集めていた。Some local volunteers were sweeping up fallen leaves with brooms. ほうきを立てかける stand a broom against ...
ほこり **dust**	ほこりを立てる stir up dust ほこりが立つ dust spreads 　物置では、少し動くだけでほこりが立った。Just slightly moving in the storeroom stirred up some dust. ほこりがたまる dust collects/accumulates 　棚の上には、分厚くほこりがたまっている。There is a thick layer of dust on the shelf. ほこりを払う dust 　ツリーをしまう前に、よくほこりを払いなさい。Dust the Christmas tree well before putting it away. ほこりをかぶる be covered with dust 　その植物の葉っぱは、すっかりほこりをかぶって

いた。The leaves of the plant were all covered with dust.

ほこりを取る remove dust

窓(ガラス)
window(pane)

窓(ガラス)を拭く wipe a window

窓(ガラス)を磨く clean a window

高層ビルの窓ガラスを磨く仕事は、私には絶対無理です。Cleaning the windows of a high-rise building would be an impossible job for me.

窓(ガラス)が曇る a window gets misted up

電車の窓はすっかり曇っていて、外が見えなかった。The windows of the train were all fogged up, so we couldn't see outside.

窓(ガラス)が割れる a window breaks

窓(ガラス)を割る break a window

窓ガラスが1枚、何者かに割られていた。Somebody had broken one of the windows.

窓がある[ない] there are windows [no windows]

窓を開ける[閉める] open [close] a window

窓をはずす remove a windowpane from a window

汚れ
dirt, stain

汚れがつく get stained

汚れが目立つ the stain is noticeable

白だと汚れが目立つから、別の色にしよう。Stains are noticeable on white, so let's choose some other color.

汚れを落とす remove dirt

汚れを洗い落とす wash off dirt

汚れが落ちる the stain comes off

この洗剤は、とにかく汚れがよく落ちる。This detergent removes dirt very well.

Cooking

味
taste

味がする taste

このチーズは、ハーブとガーリックの味がする。This cheese tastes like herbs and garlic.

味がいい［よくない］taste good [bad]

味が濃い［薄い］have a strong [weak] flavor

　このスープは、私には少し味が濃すぎる。This soup tastes a bit too strong for me.

味がわからない cannot taste anything

　風邪をひいて、何を食べても味がわからない。I have a cold, so I can't taste anything.

味がよくなる the taste improves/gets better

味が落ちる the taste gets worse

　あのレストランは、最近味が落ちたといううわさだ。I hear that the food at that restaurant has gotten worse recently.

味をつける give ... flavor

味を見る taste

圧力鍋
pressure cooker

圧力鍋を使う use a pressure cooker

　圧力鍋を使うと、調理時間をずいぶん節約できる。You can save a lot of time by cooking with a pressure cooker.

圧力鍋で調理する cook in a pressure cooker

圧力鍋の圧力を抜く release the pressure from a pressure cooker

油
oil

油を引く put some oil in

　まず、鍋に油を引いて、弱火でニンニクを炒めます。First, put some oil in a pan and fry the garlic over a low flame.

油で炒める fry

油で揚げる deep-fry

　「この魚はどうやって食べるのですか？」「油で揚げることが多いです」"How do you cook this fish?" "We usually deep-fry it."

油通しをする soak ... lightly in hot oil

　野菜に油通しをしておくと、料理が色よく仕上がる。If you soak vegetables lightly in hot oil, their colors will stay vivid when cooked.

油を拭き取る wipe the grease off

オーブン・天火 **oven**	オーブンで焼く bake ... in an oven 今、オーブンでローストチキンを焼いているところです。I'm now baking a chicken in the oven. オーブンを（…度に）予熱する／温めておく preheat the oven (to ...) オーブンを１８０℃に予熱しなさい。Preheat the oven to 180 degrees Celsius. オーブンの時間をセットする set the oven timer オーブンに入れる put ... in the oven オーブンから取り出す take ... out of the oven
オーブントースター **toaster oven**	オーブントースターで焼く toast ... in the toaster oven オーブントースターで作る make/cook ... in the toaster oven このクッキーは、オーブントースターで作れます。You can make these cookies in a toaster oven. オーブントースターで温める warm ... in the toaster oven お昼に残り物のピザをオーブントースターで温めた。I warmed up some leftover pizza in the toaster oven for lunch.
おたま・しゃもじ **ladle,** **rice paddle**	おたまですくう ladle おたまであくを取る skim the scum with a ladle しゃもじでよそう serve with a (rice) scoop しゃもじで、ごはんをよそってもらえますか？ Would you serve the rice with the rice scoop? しゃもじで混ぜる mix with a (rice) scoop 煮た具を炊きあがったごはんにしゃもじで混ぜます。You mix the cooked ingredients with cooked rice using a rice scoop.
こしょう **pepper**	こしょうをする pepper 肉にはやや強めにこしょうをしてください。Pepper the meat rather liberally. こしょうをふる sprinkle pepper こしょうをかける sprinkle pepper ラーメンにこしょうをかけようとしたら、ふたが取れてしまった。When I was going to sprinkle pepper on

the ramen, the lid came off.

ごはん
cooked rice

ごはんを炊く cook/boil rice
炊飯ジャーではなく、鍋でごはんを炊いています。I cook rice in a pot, not in a rice cooker.

ごはんを蒸らす let rice steam
スイッチが切れてから、しばらくごはんを蒸らす必要がある。You must let the rice steam for a while after the switch goes off.

ごはんをよそう serve rice
ごはんが炊き上がる the rice is cooked
ごはんを炒める fry (cooked) rice
ごはんが焦げる the rice burns

(お)米
rice

米をとぐ wash rice
「無洗米」は、米をとがずに炊くことができるように加工されたお米です。"Musenmai" is a type of rice you can cook without washing.

米を洗う wash rice
米を炒める fry rice
本格的なピラフの作り方は、米を炒めてからスープを加えて炊く。To make authentic pilaf, you fry the rice before adding the soup when cooking.

米を蒸す steam rice
(カップ・升で)米を計る measure rice (with a measuring cup)

コンロ
(cooking) stove

コンロにかける put ... on the stove
コンロから下ろす take ... off the stove
卵を加えるときは、コンロから下ろすこと。You should take the pan off the stove when adding eggs.

コンロの火をつける turn on the stove
コンロの火を絞る lower/turn down the heat
いったん沸騰したら、コンロの火を絞って 10 分ほど煮込みます。Once boiled, turn down the heat and simmer for about 10 minutes.

コンロの火を消す turn off the stove
もう少しで、コンロの火を消すのを忘れて出かけると

ころだった。I almost went out without turning off the stove.

魚
fish

魚をさばく／(三枚に)下ろす　clean a fish/clean a fish (and slice it into three parts)

彼は自分で釣った魚をさばいて、刺身を作ってくれた。He cleaned the fish he had caught himself and made sashimi.

魚の下ごしらえをする　clean a fish; prepare fish for cooking

魚を焼く　grill fish

台所に魚のにおいがこもるので、家では魚を焼きません。I don't grill fish at home because the kitchen ends up smelling like fish.

魚を煮付ける　cook fish

魚に塩をする　salt fish

魚の臭みを取るために、魚に塩をしてしばらく置きます。Salt the fish and leave it for a while in order to get rid of the fishy smell.

魚のうろこを取る　scale a fish

魚(の身)を摺る　grind (the meat of) a fish

魚が焦げる　a fish burns

塩
salt

塩をする　salt

単に塩とこしょうをしただけのステーキが、ものすごくおいしかった。The steak seasoned only with salt and pepper tasted very good.

塩を加える　add salt

スープの味を見て、足りなければ塩を加えてください。Taste the soup and add some salt if needed.

塩をふる　sprinkle salt

塩をまぶす　sprinkle salt

ゆで上がった枝豆をざるにあげて、塩をまぶした。I drained the boiled green soybeans in a colander and sprinkled on some salt.

塩をかける　sprinkle salt

塩でもむ　rub ... with salt; rub salt (into ...)

塩<ruby>塩<rt>しお</rt></ruby>がきいている be pleasantly salty

<ruby>塩<rt>しお</rt></ruby>が<ruby>足<rt>た</rt></ruby>りない be not salty enough

<ruby>塩<rt>しお</rt></ruby>を<ruby>控<rt>ひか</rt></ruby>える use less salt

<ruby>健康<rt>けんこう</rt></ruby>のために、<ruby>少<rt>すこ</rt></ruby>し<ruby>塩<rt>しお</rt></ruby>を<ruby>控<rt>ひか</rt></ruby>えるようにしています。I try to use less salt for the sake of my health.

<ruby>塩<rt>しお</rt></ruby>を<ruby>回<rt>まわ</rt></ruby>す pass salt

<ruby>醤油<rt>しょうゆ</rt></ruby>
soy sauce

<ruby>醤油<rt>しょうゆ</rt></ruby>をかける pour soy sauce on ...

アボカドとマグロを<ruby>切<rt>き</rt></ruby>ったものに<ruby>醤油<rt>しょうゆ</rt></ruby>をかけてわさびを<ruby>混<rt>ま</rt></ruby>ぜた。I poured some soy sauce on the diced avocado and tuna, then mixed in some wasabi.

<ruby>醤油<rt>しょうゆ</rt></ruby>を<ruby>加<rt>くわ</rt></ruby>える add soy sauce

<ruby>醤油<rt>しょうゆ</rt></ruby>を<ruby>垂<rt>た</rt></ruby>らす add a few drops of soy sauce

<ruby>醤油<rt>しょうゆ</rt></ruby>につける dip in soy sauce

にぎり<ruby>寿司<rt>すし</rt></ruby>は、ネタの<ruby>方<rt>ほう</rt></ruby>に<ruby>少<rt>すこ</rt></ruby>し<ruby>醤油<rt>しょうゆ</rt></ruby>をつけるといい。You should dip the side of the sushi topping in the soy sauce.

<ruby>卵<rt>たまご</rt></ruby>・<ruby>玉子<rt>たまご</rt></ruby>
egg

<ruby>卵<rt>たまご</rt></ruby>を<ruby>割<rt>わ</rt></ruby>る break/crack an egg

<ruby>片手<rt>かたて</rt></ruby>で<ruby>卵<rt>たまご</rt></ruby>を<ruby>割<rt>わ</rt></ruby>ることができますか。Can you break an egg with one hand?

<ruby>卵<rt>たまご</rt></ruby>をかき<ruby>混<rt>ま</rt></ruby>ぜる beat an egg

<ruby>卵<rt>たまご</rt></ruby>を<ruby>黄身<rt>きみ</rt></ruby>と<ruby>白身<rt>しろみ</rt></ruby>に<ruby>分<rt>わ</rt></ruby>ける separate the yolk and the white

<ruby>卵<rt>たまご</rt></ruby>を<ruby>焼<rt>や</rt></ruby>く fry an egg

<ruby>朝<rt>あさ</rt></ruby>は<ruby>大体<rt>だいたい</rt></ruby><ruby>卵<rt>たまご</rt></ruby>を<ruby>焼<rt>や</rt></ruby>いて、あとはトーストとコーヒーです。I usually fry some eggs and have some toast and coffee in the morning.

<ruby>卵<rt>たまご</rt></ruby>をゆでる boil an egg

<ruby>卵<rt>たまご</rt></ruby>を<ruby>半熟<rt>はんじゅく</rt></ruby>にする soft-boil an egg

<ruby>卵<rt>たまご</rt></ruby>をとく beat/whisk an egg

<ruby>卵<rt>たまご</rt></ruby>でとじる add a beaten egg (into vegetables, etc. to hold them together)

<ruby>卵<rt>たまご</rt></ruby>を(…に)<ruby>落<rt>お</rt></ruby>とす put an egg in ...

<ruby>卵<rt>たまご</rt></ruby>を(…に)<ruby>割<rt>わ</rt></ruby>り<ruby>入<rt>い</rt></ruby>れる break/crack an egg and put it into ...

ボウルに<ruby>卵<rt>たまご</rt></ruby>を<ruby>割<rt>わ</rt></ruby>り<ruby>入<rt>い</rt></ruby>れてよくかき<ruby>混<rt>ま</rt></ruby>ぜ、<ruby>牛乳<rt>ぎゅうにゅう</rt></ruby>を<ruby>加<rt>くわ</rt></ruby>えます。Break eggs into a bowl, beat them well, and add some milk.

卵を使う use eggs

卵を(ごはんに)かける put a beaten egg (on rice)

炒り卵をつくる scramble an egg

電子レンジ
microwave
(oven)

電子レンジに入れる put ... in the microwave

電子レンジで温める heat/warm up ... in the microwave

牛乳を電子レンジで温めたら、吹きこぼれてしまった。I heated up some milk in the microwave and it boiled over.

電子レンジでチンする heat/warm up ... in the microwave

電子レンジでチンするだけで食べられる食品をストックしてある。I have stocked up on a lot of ready-to-eat food that you only need to heat in the microwave.

電子レンジを使う use the microwave

鍋
pan, pot

鍋を火にかける put a pot on the burner

鍋を火にかけている間は、火のそばから離れないように。Don't leave the kitchen with a pot on the burner.

鍋に油を引く put some oil in the pot

鍋を火から下ろす take the pot off the stove

鍋に焦げつく burn and stick to a pan

火が強すぎたのか、肉が鍋に焦げついてしまった。The meat has burnt and stuck to the pan, maybe because the heat was too strong.

鍋で煮る cook in a pan

鍋でゆでる boil in a pan

鍋で(さっと)ゆがく blanch ... in a pan

鍋でお湯を沸かす boil water in a pan

鍋に落としぶたをする put a small lid directly on food this is cooking in a pan/pot

肉
meat

肉を切る cut meat

肉を焼く broil/grill meat; roast meat

肉を炒める fry meat

肉を炒めてから、野菜を入れてください。Fry the

meat for a while and then put in the vegetables.

肉をソテーする sauté meat

肉をミンチにする mince meat

ひき肉が売っていなかったので、自分で肉をミンチにした。They didn't have minced meat at the shop, so I minced some myself.

肉をマリネードする marinate meat

肉を巻く wrap ... with meat

アスパラガスに薄切りの肉を巻いた。I wrapped the asparagus in thin slices of meat.

バター
butter

バターを溶かす melt some butter

鍋にバターを溶かして小麦粉を入れ、牛乳で少しずつ伸ばします。Melt some butter in a saucepan and add some flour, and then gradually add milk.

バターを入れる put some butter in ...

バターで炒める fry ... in butter

タマネギが茶色になるまでバターで炒めなさい。Fry the onions in butter until they are brown.

バターでソテーする sauté ... in butter

バターを塗る spread butter

ホットケーキにバターを塗って、メープルシロップをたっぷりかけた。I spread some butter on the pancakes and poured on plenty of maple syrup.

パン
bread

パンを焼く bake bread

天然酵母を使って、パンを焼いてみた。I tried baking bread using natural yeast starter.

パンをトーストする toast some bread

パンにバターを塗る butter some bread

パンを冷凍する keep bread frozen

パンが残ったら、冷凍しておけばいい。If any bread is left, you can freeze it.

フライ返し
turner

フライ返しを使う use a turner

フライ返しでひっくり返す turn over with a turner

目玉焼きをフライ返しでひっくり返したら、黄身がつぶれた。I turned over the egg with the turner and the yolk broke.

**フライパン
(frying) pan**

フライ返しで押しつける　press with a turner

フライパンを火にかける　put a frying pan on the burner

フライパンを熱する　heat a frying pan

　コツはフライパンをよく熱して、強火で一気に炒めることだ。The trick is to heat the pan well and stir-fry the ingredients over a high flame.

フライパンに油を引く　oil a frying pan; put some oil in the frying pan

　フライパンに油を引くのを忘れたので、焦げついた。I forgot to oil the pan so the food got burnt and stuck to it.

フライパンで焼く　fry ... in a frying pan

フライパンで炒める　stir-fry ... in a frying pan

フライパンを火から下ろす　take the frying pan off the stove

**包丁
(kitchen) knife**

包丁をとぐ　sharpen a kitchen knife

　この包丁は、買ってから一度もといでいない。I haven't sharpened this knife once since I bought it.

包丁で切る　cut ... with a knife

包丁が（よく）切れる［切れない］a knife cuts well [doesn't cut well]

包丁（の背）でたたく　beat ... with the back of a knife blade

　豚肉を包丁の背でたたいて、柔らかくします。Beat the pork with the back of the knife blade until it is tender.

包丁で皮をむく　peel ... with a knife

　包丁でジャガイモの皮をむくのは、難しい。It's hard to peel potatoes with a knife.

包丁でつぶす　crush ... with a knife (by pressing on the side of the blade)

包丁で指を切る　cut one's finger with a knife

**ボウル・ざる
bowl, colander**

ボウルに入れる　put ... in a bowl

　材料をすべてボウルに入れて、よく混ぜてください。

Put all the ingredients in a bowl and mix well.

ボウルの中で混ぜる mix ... in a bowl

ボウルの中でこねる knead ... in a bowl

ボウルを重ねておく stack bowls

ざるに揚げる drain ... in a colander

そうめんをざるに揚げたら、流水でよく洗います。

Drain the *somen* noodles in a colander and wash them well under running water.

ざるで水を切る drain ... in a colander

ざるに（並べて）干す leave ... in a colander to dry

まな板
cutting board

まな板（の上）に置く／載せる put ... on a cutting board

まな板の上で切る cut ... on a cutting board

まな板を使う use a cutting board

彼女はまな板を使わずに、器用にニンジンを切った。

She cut the carrots skillfully without using a cutting board.

まな板を使い分ける use different cutting boards for different ingredients

まな板を洗う wash a cutting board

まな板を消毒する／殺菌する sterilize a cutting board

1週間に1度、まな板を殺菌するようにしています。

I sterilize the cutting board once a week.

マヨネーズ
mayonnaise

マヨネーズをかける add some mayonnaise

マヨネーズであえる mix with mayonnaise

ゆでたジャガイモとソーセージとタマネギを、マヨネーズであえたサラダです。This salad is made with boiled potatoes, sausages, and onions, and mixed with mayonnaise.

マヨネーズをつける add some mayonnaise; dip in mayonnaise

やかん・ケトル
kettle

やかんを火にかける put a kettle on the stove

やかんでお湯を沸かす boil water in a kettle

やかんでお湯を沸かすより、この電気ポットのほうが速い。It's quicker to boil water in this electric pot rather than with a kettle on the gas burner.

やかんを火から下ろす take a kettle off the stove

野菜
vegetables

野菜を洗う wash vegetables

冬場は水が冷たくて、野菜を洗うのがつらい。It's a pain to wash vegetables in cold water in winter.

野菜を切る cut vegetables

鍋物は、肉や野菜を切るだけで準備できるので、楽だ。It's easy to prepare *nabemono* since you only have to cut up meat and vegetables.

野菜を刻む chop/mince vegetables

野菜を炒める fry vegetables

野菜を煮る cook vegetables

野菜を煮込む cook vegetables well; stew/simmer vegetables

野菜を揚げる deep-fry vegetables

野菜を(…で)あえる toss vegetables

野菜をゆでる boil vegetables

野菜をゆがく blanch/parboil vegetables

野菜を添える garnish (steak, etc.) with vegetables

野菜を混ぜ合わせる mix vegetables

野菜に火を通す cook vegetables

野菜は生よりも火を通したほうが、たくさん食べられる。You can eat more cooked vegetables than raw vegetables.

料理
cooking

料理(を)する cook; do the cooking

ふだんは外食ばかりで、家ではほとんど料理をしません。I usually eat out and seldom cook at home.

料理を作る cook

料理を習う［教える］learn [teach] how to cook

料理が好き［嫌い］だ like [do not like] cooking

料理が得意［苦手］だ be good [poor] at cooking

料理が上手［下手］だ be good [poor] at cooking

彼は人に教えられるくらい料理が上手だ。He is so good at cooking that he can even teach it to others.

Eating

お茶 tea	お茶を入れる make tea
	お茶にする have tea
	ひと休みしてお茶にしましょうか？ Shall we take a break and have some tea?
	お茶をたてる prepare powdered tea
	お茶を出す serve tea
	お客さんが来ると、まずお茶を出してもてなすのが習慣だ。It's customary to welcome guests by serving them tea.
	お茶を飲む drink/have tea
	お茶を注ぐ pour tea
	（ごはんに）お茶をかける pour tea on rice
おなか stomach	おなかがすく become hungry
	今朝は朝ごはんを食べそこなったので、おなかがすいた。I'm hungry because I missed breakfast this morning.
	おなかがいっぱいだ be full; one's stomach is full
	ありがとうございます。もうおなかいっぱいです。Thank you, but I'm full.
	おなかがぺこぺこだ be starving
	おなかが鳴る one's stomach growls with hunger
	しーんとしたエレベーターの中で、おなかが鳴ってはずかしかった。I was embarrassed when my stomach growled in the quiet elevator.
	おなかに入れる eat (lightly)
	練習を始める前に、何かおなかに入れておかないともたないよ。You won't have enough energy unless you eat something before the practice.
おやつ・お菓子 snacks, sweets	おやつを食べる have/eat some snacks
	おやつをつまむ pick at snacks
	仕事中についつい、おやつをつまんでしまう。I can't help picking at snacks while at work.
	おやつを差し入れる give ... some snacks to eat

おやつを出す serve some snacks

ごはん・おかず
rice, food

ごはんを食べる eat/have rice; have a meal

ごはんを残す leave some rice

あまりに大盛りだったので、ごはんを残してしまった。It was such a large helping of rice that I couldn't finish it.

ごはんを平らげる eat/finish up the rice

子供たちはみな、きれいにごはんを平らげた。All the children finished up the rice.

ごはんをお代わりする have a second helping of rice

その店では、無料でごはんをお代わりすることができる。You can have a free second helping of rice at that restaurant.

ごはんを抜く skip a meal

ごはんをつぐ serve rice

ごはんにありつく (manage to) get a meal

ごはんをこぼす spill rice

ごはんを温める heat/warm up rice

皿・茶碗
dish, bowl

皿を並べる set the table; arrange the plates

皿を洗う do/wash the dishes

皿を拭く dry the dishes

私がお皿を洗うから、それを拭いてもらえますか。I'll do the dishes, so will you dry them?

皿を重ねる stack the dishes

皿を割る break a dish

高級な6枚組のセットのお皿を1枚割ってしまった。I accidentally broke a plate from the expensive six-piece set.

皿に盛りつける put ... on a dish

茶碗によそう／つぐ put (rice) into a bowl

食事
meal

食事をとる have a meal; eat

食事に気を付ける be careful about what one eats

何か食事で気を付けていることはありますか? Is there anything you are careful about when eating?

食事を終える／済ませる finish one's meal

食事を抜く　skip a meal

食事を作る　cook a meal

うちでは姉と交代で食事を作っています。My sister and I take turns cooking meals.

食事に招く　invite to a meal

お食事に招いていただいて、どうもありがとうございます。Thank you very much for inviting me to the meal.

食事に出る　go out for a meal

すみません、彼は今食事に出ています。Sorry, he's gone out for a meal now.

食事に連れていく　take ... out for a meal

食事にする　have a meal; eat

食事に誘う　ask someone to have a meal together

食事の支度をする　prepare a meal

食欲
appetite

食欲がある　have an appetite

食欲がない　have no appetite

風邪をひいていて食欲がない。I have a cold, so I have no appetite.

食欲が出る　work up one's appetite

熱が下がって、食欲が出てきた。My fever went down and I regained my appetite.

食欲がなくなる　lose one's appetite

食欲をなくす　lose one's appetite

食欲をそそる　stimulate one's appetite

このにおいは、かなり食欲をそそるね。This aroma really stimulates my appetite.

食欲がわく　one's appetite increases

食欲を減退させる　spoil/ruin one's appetite

この映画は食欲を減退させるから、食事前には見ない方がいい。Don't watch this movie before a meal because it will spoil your appetite.

食器
tableware

食器を洗う　do/wash the dishes

食器を並べる　arrange the dishes; set the table

食器を片づける　put the dishes away

食器をしまう put the dishes in (the cupboard, etc.)

ふだん使っている食器を、食器棚にしまうことはほとんどない。I seldom put the dishes I use every day in the cupboard.

朝食・昼食・夕食・夜食
breakfast, lunch, dinner, supper

朝食をとる have breakfast

いつも会社の近くのマクドナルドで、朝食をとっています。I always have breakfast at a McDonald's near my office.

朝食を食べる have breakfast

明日は午後から健康診断なので、朝食を食べないようにと言われた。I was told not to have breakfast tomorrow since I have a medical checkup in the afternoon.

朝食を抜く skip breakfast

朝食を食べ損ねる miss breakfast

朝食を準備する prepare breakfast

目が覚めたら、すでに朝食を準備してくれていた。When I woke up, he had already prepared breakfast for me.

朝食を軽くする have a light breakfast

出前・デリバリー
delivery service

出前をとる have ... delivered

「すごく疲れたから、料理したくないわ」「お寿司の出前でもとろうか？」"I'm so tired, I don't feel like cooking." "Then let's have some sushi delivered."

出前を頼む order ... by home delivery service

出前で（食事を）済ませる have a meal delivered

はし・フォーク
chopsticks, fork

はしを使う use chopsticks

はしを使いこなす use chopsticks well

日本食は今や世界中でとてもポピュラーなので、はしを使いこなす外国人はたくさんいる。Now that Japanese food is very popular around the world, there are many people who can use chopsticks very well.

はしを持つ hold chopsticks

はしを置く finish eating

はしで混ぜる mix using chopsticks

はしで切る cut with chopsticks
この肉は、はしで切れるくらい柔らかい。This meat is so tender that you can even cut it with chopsticks.

はしでつまむ pick up ... with chopsticks

はしが進む have a good appetite
みんな料理が気に入ったのか、はしが進むようだった。They seemed to like the food and have a good appetite.

はしをつける start eating; help oneself to the food
彼は出された食事に、はしをつけようともしなかった。He didn't even touch the meal that was served.

ふた
lid

ふたを取る take a lid off

ふたを開ける open; take a lid off

ふたが開く the lid opens
どうしてもこのびんのふたが開かないの。開けてもらえる？The lid of this jar just won't open. Will you help me?

ふたが開いている be open

ふたをする put a lid on
肉の片面が焼けたらふたをして、5分間蒸し焼きにします。When one side of the meat is nice and brown, put the lid on and leave it for five minutes.

ふたを閉める close; put a lid on
きっちりふたを閉めておかないと、中のものがしけってしまう。If you don't close the lid tightly, what's inside will get damp.

水・(お)湯
water, hot water

水で薄める water down; dilute ... with water

水に溶ける dissolve in water

水を足す／加える add water

水洗いする wash ... in water

水を切る drain water

水を張る fill up with water

水に漬ける soak in water
一晩水に漬けて塩を抜く soak ... in water overnight to reduce saltiness

お湯を沸かす boil water

　ちょうどコーヒーを入れようと、お湯を沸かしていたところです。 I just happened to be boiling some water to make coffee.

お湯に溶かす／お湯で溶く dissolve ... in hot water

お湯でゆでる boil in hot water

　スパゲッティは、たっぷりのお湯でゆでてください。 Boil the spaghetti in plenty of water.

Comfort & Relaxation

(インター)ネット
(Inter)net

ネットをする surf the Internet

ネットに接続する connect to the Internet

ネットで検索する search for ... on the Internet

ネットで配信する distribute ... over the Internet

　CD を買うより、ネットで配信されている音楽をダウンロードするほうが、圧倒的に多い。 I download music distributed over the Internet far more often than I buy CDs.

ネットで買う／買い物をする buy online

　最近は、本や DVD はたいていネットで買っている。 Recently, I buy most of my books and DVDs online.

ネットで予約する make a reservation through the Internet

ネットで調べる search for ... on the Internet

　大体のことはネットで調べられる。 You can search for almost anything on the Internet.

ネットで売る sell online

コーヒー
coffee

コーヒーをいれる make coffee

　キッチンから、コーヒーをいれるいいにおいがしてきた。 The nice aroma of coffee came from the kitchen.

コーヒーを沸かす brew coffee

コーヒーを飲む drink coffee

　朝、コーヒーを飲まないと 1 日が始まらない。 I can't

start a day without coffee in the morning.

コーヒー豆を煎る roast coffee beans

コーヒー豆を挽く grind coffee beans

雑誌
magazine

雑誌を読む read a magazine

雑誌を拾い読みする browse through a magazine

雑誌をめくる flip through a magazine

　雑誌をぱらぱらめくっていたら、知っている顔が目に飛び込んできた。I was flipping through a magazine when a familiar face caught my eye.

雑誌を買う buy a magazine

雑誌を立ち読みする browse through a magazine

　雑誌はあまり買わずに、立ち読みすることが多い。I don't buy magazines often; I just browse.

雑誌が溜まる magazines accumulate/pile up

雑誌を購読する／取る subscribe to a magazine

散歩
walk

散歩（を）する take a walk

　このごろは、以前より公園を散歩する人が増えた。More people take walks in the park than before.

散歩させる walk (a dog, etc.)

　朝晩 2 回、犬を散歩させています。I walk my dog twice daily, in the morning and in the evening.

散歩に行く go for a walk

散歩に出かける go out for a walk

時間
time

時間がたつ／過ぎる time passes (by)

　このごろは、時間がたつのが恐ろしく速い。Time passes by awfully fast these days.

時間をつぶす kill time

　商店街をぶらぶらして、時間をつぶした。I killed time strolling along the shopping street.

時間をかける take time; spend plenty of time

時間がある have time

　近頃は忙しくて、映画を観に行く時間がほとんどありません。I'm so busy these days that I have little time to go and see a movie.

時間がかかる it takes time (to do ...)

台所と居間を掃除するのに、すごく時間がかかった。

It took me a lot of time to clean the kitchen and the living room.

時間を費やす spend time

時間を過ごす spend time

時間を決める set a time

時間を合わせる set a clock

時間を守る be punctual

時間を変更する change the (agreed) time

時間を無駄にする waste time

時間を節約する save time

時間が余る have (an hour, etc.) left over; have extra time

時間に追われている be pressed for time

時間に追われる毎日から、しばらく逃げ出したい。

I want to escape from everyday life and the demands it places on my time.

時間に縛られる have a tight schedule

情報
information

情報を集める collect/gather information

その国について、できるだけ情報を集めないといけない。I need to collect as much information as possible about that country.

情報を交換する exchange information

友人たちと定期的に会って、情報を交換しています。I meet with my friends on a regular basis to exchange information.

情報を流す give/spread information

情報を公開する disclose information

情報を引き出す retrieve information

情報を得る get information

彼がどこからそんな情報を得ているのかは、知りません。I don't know where he gets such information.

情報を手に入れる get/obtain information

情報が広まる information spreads

その情報は、あっという間に世界中に広まった。The information spread all over the world in no time.

新聞 newspaper	情報が入ってくる news comes in
	新聞を読む read a newspaper
	新聞を取る／購読する subscribe to a newspaper
	何新聞を取っていますか？ What newspaper do you read?
	新聞を買う buy a newspaper
	新聞に目を通す look through the paper
	今朝は、新聞に目を通す暇がなかった。I didn't have time to look through the paper this morning.
	新聞に出ている be in the paper
	その新刊の広告が、今日の新聞に出ていたよ。The ad for the new book was in today's paper.
	新聞（の記事）を切り抜く clip an article from a newspaper
テレビ・ラジオ TV, radio	テレビを見る watch TV
	ラジオを聴く listen to the radio
	テレビ／ラジオをつける［消す］turn on [off] the TV/radio
	やや強い地震があったので、すぐにテレビをつけた。I felt a rather big earthquake, so I turned the TV on right away.
	テレビのチャンネルを変える change TV channels
	テレビの音量／ボリュームを上げる［下げる］turn up [down] the TV
	テレビに出る appear on TV
	あのタレントは、最近よくテレビに出ている。That celebrity often appears on TV recently.
ニュース news	ニュースを聞く hear the news
	朝は、ラジオでニュースを聞きながら、支度をします。In the morning, I get ready while listening to the news on the radio.
	ニュースが流れる news spreads
	ニュースをやっている news is broadcast
	どのチャンネルでも、その事故のニュースをやっていた。The news about the accident was broadcast

on every channel.

番組
program

ニュースを見る watch the news

番組を見る watch a TV program

番組を見逃す miss a program

番組を録画する record a program

　このハードディスクレコーダーは、自動で自分好みの番組を録画できる。This hard disk recorder can automatically record your favorite programs.

暇
(spare) time

暇がある［ない］have (free) time [no time]

暇を持て余す have too much time to kill

　仕事を辞めてから、暇を持て余しています。I have too much time to kill since I quit the job.

暇に飽かせる／任せる make use of one's free time

　暇に飽かせて"LOST"のDVDをシーズン1から5まで一気に見た。I took advantage of my free time and watched *Lost* DVDs from season 1 through 5.

暇をつぶす kill time

暇になる become free; come to have a lot of time

暇を活用する make use of one's free time

ブログ
blog

ブログに書く write in one's blog

ブログを読む read a blog

ブログを更新する update one's blog; keep one's blog updated

　彼はこの1か月の間、1日も休まずにブログを更新している。He's been keeping his blog updated for a month without a break.

ブログを始める start one's (own) blog

　80歳の祖母が、なんとブログを始めた。Amazingly, my 80-year-old grandmother started her own blog.

本
book

本を買う buy a book

本を読む read a book

本を借りる borrow a book

本を貸す lend a book

本を開く［閉じる］open [close] a book

本を読み直す／読み返す read a book again; reread a

book

昔読んだ本を今読み直すと、新しい発見があるものだ。You'll find something new if you reread a book you have read before.

本を読んで聞かせる read a book to a child, etc.
子どもの頃、母は毎日のように本を読んで聞かせてくれた。When I was small, my mother read books to me almost every day.

本をコピーする make a copy of a book

本を注文する order a book
アマゾンで本を注文したら、翌日届いた。I ordered a book from Amazon and received it the next day.

メール
e-mail

メール(を)する e-mail; send an e-mail

メールを送る send an e-mail

メールが来る receive/get an e-mail
小学校のときの友達から、メールが来て驚いた。I was surprised to receive an e-mail from a friend from my elementary school.

メールを転送する forward an e-mail
メールを携帯に転送するように、パソコンを設定してある。I have set the computer to forward my e-mails to my cell phone.

メールに返信する respond to an e-mail

メールに添付する attach to an e-mail

メールを消す delete an e-mail

メールを保存する save an e-mail

Furniture

椅子
chair

椅子に座る sit on/in a chair

椅子に(腰)掛ける／腰を下ろす sit on a chair

椅子から転げ落ちる fall off a chair
笑いすぎて、もう少しで椅子から転げ落ちるところだった。I laughed so hard that I almost fell off the

chair.

椅子から立ち上がる rise from one's chair

部屋に入ると、彼は椅子から立ち上がってあいさつ
してくれた。When I walked into the room, he got up
from his chair and greeted me.

椅子を引く draw/pull up a chair

そこはウェイターが椅子を引いて座らせてくれる
高級レストランだった。It was an exclusive restaurant where the waiter draws up a chair for you.

椅子を引き寄せる draw/pull up a chair

椅子(の高さ)を調節する adjust a chair

椅子を勧める offer someone a chair; invite someone to
sit down

**押し入れ・
クローゼット
closet**

押し入れにしまう store ... in the closet

ふとんは毎日たたんで、押し入れにしまっています。
Every day I fold up the futon and store it in the closet.

押し入れに入れる put ... in the closet

押し入れに押し込む stuff ... in the closet

部屋中に散乱していた洋服や雑誌を、全部押し
入れに押し込んだ。I picked up all the clothes and
magazines scattered around the room and stuffed
them in the closet.

押し入れから出す take ... out of the closet

押し入れを換気する air out the closet

たまに押し入れを換気しないと、中がかびくさくな
る。You should air out the closet once in a while, or
it will smell musty inside.

**カーテン
curtain**

カーテンをかける／吊るす hang/put up the curtains

まだ引っ越したばかりで、カーテンさえかけていま
せん。I just moved into the place and haven't even
put up the curtains.

カーテンを引く draw/pull the curtains

カーテンを開ける open/draw back/pull back the curtains

カーテンを開けたら、外は一面の銀世界だった。I
opened the curtains and found that the outside was

all covered with snow.

カーテンを閉める close/draw/pull the curtains

カーテンを下ろす pull down the curtain

鍵
lock, key

鍵をかける／閉める lock

彼はちょっとした外出のときは、鍵をかけない。He doesn't lock the door when he goes out for a short while.

鍵を開ける unlock

鍵がかかる it locks

このドアは自動的に鍵がかかるので、締め出されないように気をつけること。This door locks automatically, so be careful not to lock yourself out.

鍵がかかっている be locked

その引き出しは鍵がかかっていて、何が入っているのかわからない。The drawer is locked and I don't know what's inside.

鍵を差し込む insert a key (into a keyhole)

鍵を回す turn a key

鍵を渡す hand/give a key (to someone)

（合）鍵を作る make a (duplicate) key

じゅうたん・
カーペット
carpet

じゅうたんを敷く lay/put down a carpet

畳の部屋にじゅうたんを敷くのは、あまり勧められない。I don't recommend laying a carpet in a tatami room.

じゅうたんを敷き詰める spread a carpet across the floor

じゅうたんにしみをつける stain a carpet

誰かがワインをこぼして、じゅうたんにしみをつけてしまった。Someone spilled wine and stained the carpet.

じゅうたんを洗う clean a carpet

じゅうたんを替える change a carpet

ソファ
sofa

ソファに座る sit on a sofa

私がソファに座ると、すぐに犬がやってきて隣に飛び乗る。Every time I sit on the sofa, my dog jumps on next to me.

ソファに寝そべる lie down on a sofa

ソファに横になる lie down on a sofa

　ソファに横になったら、そのまま朝まで眠ってしまった。

I lay down on the sofa and slept there till morning.

ソファで寝る sleep on a sofa

**テーブル・
食卓
table**

テーブルを置く set out a table

テーブルに着く sit at the table; take one's seat at the table

　みんながテーブルに着いたら、乾杯しよう。Let's make a toast when everyone sits down at the table.

テーブルのセッティングをする set the table

テーブルに（料理を）並べる put (the food) on the table

　テーブルに料理を並べるのを手伝ってくれる？ Will you help me put the food on the table?

**ドア・戸
door**

ドアを開ける［閉める］open [close/shut] a door

ドアが開く a door opens

　急にドアが開いたので、頭をぶつけそうになった。

I almost hit my head on the door when it suddenly opened.

ドアが閉まる a door closes/shuts

　ドアが閉まらないように、押さえていてもらえますか？

Would you hold the door so that it doesn't close?

ドアをノックする knock on a door

　誰かが隣の部屋のドアをノックする音が聞こえた。

I heard someone knock on the next door.

ドアを（激しく）たたく bang on a door

ドアに指をはさむ catch one's finger in a door

ドアをこじ開ける pry a door open

ドアに鍵をかける lock the door

ドアを開け放す leave the door (wide) open

**時計
watch, clock**

時計を（壁に）掛ける hang a clock (on the wall)

時計を見る look at a watch/clock

　彼はちらちら時計を見ていたので、何か用事があったのかもしれない。He kept looking at his watch, so he might have had something to do.

時計を合わせる set a watch/clock

時計が進む a watch/clock gains

大丈夫、その時計は10分進んでいるから、終電には間に合うよ。Don't worry, that clock is 10 minutes fast. You'll make the last train.

時計を（1時間）進める move a watch/clock forward (an hour); set a watch/clock an hour ahead

明日から夏時間になるから、全部の時計を1時間進めなきゃ。We have to move all the clocks forward an hour since daylight savings time starts tomorrow.

時計が遅れる a watch/clock loses

私の腕時計は5分遅れているから、今は5時ちょうどだ。My watch is five minutes slow, so the actual time is five sharp.

時計を（1時間）遅らせる move a watch/clock backward (an hour); set a watch/clock an hour behind

時計が止まる a watch/clock stops

時計が壊れる a watch/clock breaks

時計を修理する repair a watch/clock

時計が読める be able to tell the time

娘は3歳ですが、もう時計が読めます。My daughter is three, but she is already able to tell the time.

（腕）時計をつける／する［はずす］wear/put on [take off] one's watch

時計（の針）が3時を指す the clock/watch shows (three)

ハンガー
hanger

ハンガーにかける put ... on a hanger

脱いだ上着をハンガーにかけて、しばらく風をあてた。I took off my jacket and put it on a hanger to air it out.

ハンガーに吊るす put ... on a hanger

ハンガーで干す let ... dry on a hanger

ふとん
futon, quilted bedding

ふとんを敷く spread/lay out a futon

私は畳の部屋に、ふとんを敷いて寝ています。I sleep on a futon, which I lay out in a room with tatami.

ふとんをたたむ fold up a futon

ふとんを上げる put away a futon (in the closet)

ふとんを上げ下げする take out and put away a futon

年を取ると、ふとんを上げ下げするのがきつい。When you get old, it's hard to take out and put away your futon.

ふとんを干す air (out) a futon

ベランダでふとんを干した。I hung the futons on the balcony to air them out.

ふとんを掛ける cover with a futon

ふとんにくるまる cover oneself up in a futon

こう寒いと、ふとんにくるまって、1日中ごろごろしていたくなる。When it is this cold, I feel like wrapping myself up in a futon and lying around all day.

ふとんに横になる／寝転ぶ lie down on a futon

休日にはふとんに寝転んで、のんびり本を読む。I lounge around in bed and leisurely read books on weekends.

ふとんを打ち直してもらう have the (cotton) stuffing of a futon repacked

ふとんにカバーをかける put a cover over a futon

**ブラインド
blinds, shades**

ブラインドを下ろす pull down the shades

あの窓はいつもブラインドが下ろされている。The blinds of that window are always lowered.

ブラインドを下げる pull down the shades

ブラインドを上げる pull/draw up the shades

**ベッド
bed**

ベッドを整える make one's bed

子どものころに、自分でベッドを整えるようにしつけられた。I was taught to make my bed by myself when I was small.

ベッドに寝る sleep in a bed

ベッドに寝そべる lie down on a bed

ベッドに寝そべって、漫画を読む read comics in bed

ベッドに横になる lie in bed; lie down on a bed

ベッドに潜り込む crawl into bed

とても疲れていたので、家に着くとそのままベッドに潜り込んだ。I was so tired that I crawled into bed right after I got home.

ベッドがきしむ a bed creaks

ベッドから転げ落ちる fall out of bed

ベッドから飛び起きる spring/leap out of bed

目が覚めて時計を見たとたん、ベッドから飛び起きた。I woke up, looked at the clock, and then sprang out of bed.

目覚まし(時計)
alarm clock

目覚ましをかける set the alarm (clock)

6時に目覚ましをかけたはずなのに、鳴らなかった。I thought I had set the alarm for six, but it never went off.

目覚ましをセットする set the alarm (clock)

目覚ましを止める stop/turn off the alarm

知らないうちに目覚ましを止めていたらしく、起きたらもう11時だった。I must have turned off the alarm without knowing it, because I woke up to find it was already 11.

目覚ましが鳴る the alarm goes off

Electrical Appliances

アイロン
iron

アイロンをかける iron; press

ふだん着るものには、ほとんどアイロンをかけない。I seldom iron the clothes I wear every day.

アイロンを当てる iron; press

アイロンで(しわを)伸ばす iron out (the wrinkles)

アイロンがいらない do not need ironing; non-iron

この素材はしわにならないので、アイロンがいりません。This material doesn't need ironing since it never wrinkles.

アイロンで焦がす burn ... while ironing

エアコン
air conditioner

エアコンをつける[消す] turn on [off] the air conditioner

エアコンをつけたまま寝たら、のどが痛くなった。I

slept with the air conditioner on, so I've got a sore throat.

エアコンのタイマーをかける set the timer on the air conditioner

1時間後に切れるように、エアコンのタイマーをかけた。 I set the timer so that the air conditioner will turn off in an hour.

エアコンの設定温度を上げる［下げる］raise [lower] the temperature of the air conditioner

エアコンの温度を調節する adjust the temperature of the air conditioner

乾燥機 (clothes) dryer

乾燥機にかける put ... in a dryer

このセーターを乾燥機にかけたら、縮んでしまった。 I dried this sweater in the dryer and it shrank.

乾燥機で乾かす dry ... in a dryer

乾燥機を回す use a (clothes) dryer

蛍光灯 fluorescent light

蛍光灯がちかちかする a fluorescent light blinks

蛍光灯がちかちかするようになってきたら、そろそろ取り換え時だ。 It's time to change the fluorescent lights when they start blinking.

蛍光灯がちらつく a fluorescent light blinks

蛍光灯がつかない a fluorescent light doesn't go on

蛍光灯が切れる a fluorescent light goes out

蛍光灯がまぶしい a fluorescent light is bright

蛍光灯はまぶしすぎるので、居間では白熱灯を使っている。 Fluorescent lights are too bright, so I use incandescent lamps in the living room.

蛍光灯を取り換える change fluorescent lights

スイッチ switch

スイッチを入れる turn on (the switch); switch on

暗闇の中、手探りで電気のスイッチを入れた。 I groped for the switch in the dark and turned it on.

スイッチを切る turn off (the switch); switch off

スイッチを押す press a switch

スイッチが入って［切れて］いる be (turned) on [off]

このDVDレコーダーは、ダビングが終わると自動的

にスイッチが切れる。This DVD recorder automatically turns off when it finishes dubbing.

炊飯器
rice cooker

炊飯器で炊く cook in a rice cooker

炊飯器のタイマーをセットする set the timer on the rice cooker

昨日の夜、炊飯器のタイマーをセットするのを忘れていた。I forgot to set the timer on the rice cooker last night.

炊飯器のスイッチを入れる turn on the rice cooker

炊飯器で保温する keep ... warm in the rice cooker

洗濯機
washing
machine

洗濯機に入れる put ... in the washing machine

洗濯機で洗う wash ... in the washing machine; machine-wash

このダウンジャケットは、洗濯機で洗える。This down jacket is machine-washable.

洗濯機を回す use the washing machine

洗濯物が大量にたまっていたので、今日は洗濯機を 3 回も回した。I had a lot of things to wash, so I used the washing machine three times today.

掃除機
vacuum cleaner

掃除機をかける vacuum; use the vacuum cleaner

犬を飼っているので、毎日掃除機をかけないと、部屋が大変なことになる。I have a dog so I have to use the vacuum every day, otherwise the apartment becomes a mess.

掃除機を使う use the vacuum cleaner

掃除機を買い替える buy a new vacuum cleaner to replace an old one

タイマー
timer

タイマーをセットする set the timer

タイマーを 9 分にセットして、スパゲッティをゆで始めた。I set the timer for nine minutes and started boiling the spaghetti.

タイマーを入れる set the timer

タイマーが切れる something automatically goes off at the set time

電球
light bulb

電球が切れる a light bulb burns out
　トイレの電球が切れたので、新しい電球を買いに行った。The light bulb in the toilet burned out, so I went to buy a new one.
電球がつかない a light bulb doesn't go on
電球を取り換える／付け替える change light bulbs
　私は天井に手が届かないのですが、電球を取り換えてもらえませんか? I can't reach the ceiling, so could you change the light bulbs for me?

電灯・電気・
明かり
electric light

電灯／電気／明かりをつける turn on the lights
明かりがともる be lit up
　街の明かりがともった。The town is lit up.
電灯／電気を(こまめに)消す turn off the lights (often)
　使っていない部屋の電気を、こまめに消すようにしよう。I'll try to turn off the lights as often as possible in the rooms that are not used.
電灯を取り付ける install an electric light
明かりを暗くする dim the lights
電気が点滅する the light blinks
電気がつけっぱなしだ the lights are left on
　電気をつけっぱなしにしたまま、眠りこんでしまった。I fell asleep with the lights on.
電気が流れる electricity is running; be electrified
電気を節約する save electricity

電話・携帯電話
telephone,
cell phone

電話(を)する／かける call; make a (phone) call
電話がかかる get/receive a (phone) call
　顔は知っているが一度も話したことのない同僚から、電話がかかってきた。I got a call from a coworker I have seen before but never spoken to.
電話をとる answer the phone; pick up the receiver
電話を切る hang up
電話をかけ直す call again; call back
　忙しそうだね。また後で電話をかけ直すよ。You sound busy. I'll call you back later.
電話が遠い can't hear ... on the line

電話(のベル)が鳴る a telephone rings

シャワーを浴びていて、電話が鳴っているのに気がつかなかった。 I was taking a shower, so I didn't notice the telephone ringing.

電話に出る answer the phone/call

今、手が離せないの。代わりに電話に出てくれる？ I'm really busy now. Would you answer the phone for me?

電話がつながる get through to ...; reach ... by phone

昨日からずっとかけていたのだが、ようやく彼女に電話がつながった。 I've been trying to call her since yesterday, and I finally reached her.

電話がある there is a phone (call)

山田君から電話があった。 I had a phone call from Yamada.

このへんには公衆電話がない。 There are no pay phones around here.

電話を引く have a phone (line) installed

自宅に電話を引いていますか？ Have you got a landline at home?

留守番電話にメッセージを残す leave a message on the answering machine

電話で話す talk over the phone

電話で申し込む apply by phone

電話が通じる get through to ...; reach ... by phone

電話で呼び出す call someone up by phone

電話で通報する report to the police by phone

冷蔵庫
refrigerator

冷蔵庫を開ける［閉める］ open [close/shut] the refrigerator

冷蔵庫に入れる put ... in the refrigerator

ピザが残ったら、ラップをして冷蔵庫に入れておいてね。 If there's any pizza left, wrap it up and put it in the refrigerator.

冷蔵庫から出す take ... out of the refrigerator

Incidents & Accidents

エアコン
air conditioner

エアコンがつかない the air conditioner doesn't work

エアコンがつかないんですが、修理に来てもらえますか。The air conditioner doesn't work. Can you come to fix it?

エアコンが壊れている the air conditioner is broken

エアコンを修理する repair/fix an air conditioner

入居するまでには必ずエアコンを修理しておいてください。Please make sure to fix the air conditioner before I move in.

エアコンが強すぎる the temperature is set too low

エアコンがきいていない the air conditioner is not working sufficiently

鍵
lock, key

鍵をなくす lose one's key

どこで鍵をなくしたのか、全くわかりません。I have no idea where I lost my key.

鍵を落とす lose/drop one's key

鍵をかけ忘れる／締め忘れる forget to lock

鍵を替える change a lock

部屋を借りるときは、ドアの鍵を替えてもらったほうがいい。You should request that the lock be changed when you rent an apartment.

騒音
noise

騒音がひどい the noise is terrible

私のアパートは大きな通りに面しているため、自動車の騒音がひどい。Since my apartment faces a big street, the traffic noise is terrible.

騒音を遮断する block out noise

騒音がやむ the noise stops

電気
lights, electricity

電気が消える the lights go out

電気がつかない the lights don't turn on

電気のブレーカーが落ちる the circuit breaker shuts off

エアコンとオーブンとドライヤーを同時に使うと、電気のブレーカーが落ちる。The circuit breaker shuts off if I use the air conditioner, the oven, and the hair dryer at the same time.

電気が漏れる／漏電する short-circuit

電気を食う consume a lot of electricity

オイルヒーターは、思ったより電気を食う。Oil heaters consume more electricity than I expected.

天井
ceiling

天井から雨漏りする leak from the ceiling

天井を這う crawl on the ceiling

天井を虫が這っている。A bug is crawling on the ceiling.

トイレ
toilet

トイレが詰まっている the toilet is blocked/clogged up

トイレの水が流れない the toilet doesn't flush

トイレが水漏れする water leaks from the toilet

昨日からトイレが水漏れしています。Water has been leaking from the toilet since yesterday.

（不注意で）トイレに物を流す drop something in the toilet and flush it by mistake

DAILY LIFE

The Weather

雨（あめ）
rain

雨が降る it rains

雨が降り始める／降り出す it begins raining

雨になる it gets rainy

この分だと、夕方には雨になるかもしれない。Judging from the sky, it might rain in the evening.

雨が上がる the rain stops

映画館を出るころには、雨は上がっていた。The rain had stopped when I left the movie theater.

雨が止む the rain stops

あと少ししたら、雨は止むだろう。It will stop raining before long.

雨が（降り）続く it continues to rain; it keeps raining

ここ1週間、ずっと雨が続いています。It has been raining for a week.

雨が多い［少ない］have much [little] rain

シアトルは雨が多い。It rains a lot in Seattle.

雨に降られる be caught in the rain

雨に洗われる be washed (clean) by the rain

雨に洗われた木々の緑が美しい。The leaves of the trees look all the more beautiful after a rainfall.

風（かぜ）
wind

風が吹く the wind blows

風が強い it's windy; the wind is strong

風が強くて、洗濯物が飛ばされてしまった。The strong wind blew some of the laundry away.

風が強まる［弱まる］the wind gets stronger [weaker]

午後になって、だんだん風が強まってきた。The wind got stronger in the afternoon.

風が出てくる the wind picks up

風が止む the wind stops

風が吹きつける the wind blows hard

風が凪ぐ／治まる the wind dies down

風が治まるまで、船は出ないとのことです。 They say that the ferry will not leave unless the wind dies down.

風向きが変わる the direction of the wind shifts

気温
temperature

気温が高い［低い］ the temperature is high [low]

湿度が低いから、気温が高いわりに快適だ。 It's fairly comfortable despite the high temperature, thanks to the low humidity.

気温が上がる／上昇する［下がる］ the temperature gets higher [lower]; the temperature goes up [down]

ここ数日で、ぐっと気温が下がってきた。 It has been getting much colder over the last few days.

気温が…に達する the temperature will reach ...

熊谷では今日、気温が３９度に達したらしい。 I hear the temperature reached 39 degrees in Kumagaya today.

気温の変動が激しい there have been major changes in temperature

最近は気温の変動が激しいので、体調管理が難しい。 It's difficult to maintain your health since the temperature has been changing so much these days.

霧
fog, mist

霧が出る it gets foggy

朝、このあたりはよく霧が出ます。 It often gets foggy in the morning around here.

霧が立つ fog rises (as from a valley)

霧がかかる it is foggy

霧がかかっていたので、残念ながら富士山を見ることはできなかった。 Unfortunately, we couldn't see Mt. Fuji because of the fog.

霧が深い the fog is thick/heavy/dense; it is very foggy

霧が濃くなる the fog gets thicker

霧が濃くなってきたから、運転には気をつけて。
The fog is getting thicker, so drive carefully.

霧が晴れる the fog lifts/clears up

昼前には、すっきりと霧が晴れた。The fog cleared up before noon.

霧が立ち込める be shrouded in a fog

あたり一面、霧が立ち込めていた。There was fog all around.

霧に包まれる be enveloped in fog

霧が流れる the fog moves

台風
typhoon

台風が発生する a typhoon forms

昨日、フィリピンのほうで、台風が発生したらしい。It seems a typhoon formed near the Philippines yesterday.

台風が近づく／接近する a typhoon approaches

台風が近づいているから、今日は早く家に帰ったほうがいい。We should go home early today since the typhoon is approaching.

台風が…に上陸する a typhoon hits/strikes …

台風は今朝、紀伊半島に上陸した。The typhoon hit the Kii Peninsula this morning.

台風の目に入る the eye of a typhoon passes over …

台風の目に入ると、雨も風もぴたっと止む。When the eye of a typhoon is passing, the rain and wind come to a halt.

台風が過ぎる／去る a typhoon passes

台風が過ぎた後は、晴天になることが多い。After a typhoon passes, it usually clears up.

台風が来る a typhoon comes

台風がそれる a typhoon goes off the predicted path

台風がそれてくれればいいのだけど。I hope the typhoon will move off the expected course.

台風が発達する a typhoon develops

太陽
the sun

太陽が昇る［沈む］the sun rises [sets]; the sun goes up [down]

太陽が昇る1時間前に、山小屋を出発しました。
We left the lodge an hour before the sun went up.

太陽が出ている it is sunny

今日は太陽が出ていないから、少し肌寒い。It's kind of chilly since the sun is not out today.

太陽が輝く the sun shines

太陽が照りつける the sun blazes down

梅雨
rainy season

梅雨に入る the rainy season starts

先週、梅雨に入ったらしい。I hear the rainy season started last week.

梅雨が明ける the rainy season ends

やっと梅雨が明けた。The rainy season is finally over.

梅雨が長引く the rainy season drags on

今年はいつもの年より、梅雨が長引いている。This year, the rainy season is lasting longer than usual.

天気
weather

天気がいい it's sunny/clear; the weather is good

天気が悪い the weather is bad

天気になる the weather clears up

明日、天気になりますように。I hope the weather will be good tomorrow.

天気は下り坂だ the weather will turn for the worse

予報によると、天気は下り坂だそうだ。According to the forecast, the weather will turn for the worse.

天気が崩れる the weather worsens

天気が変わる the weather changes

今日は目まぐるしく天気が変わった。The weather kept changing rapidly today.

天気が変わりやすい the weather is changeable

天気がぐずつく the weather remains unsettled; it will rain on and off

天気がぐずついて、洗濯物がなかなか乾かない。The laundry won't quite dry because the weather won't stay sunny enough.

天気が急変する the weather changes suddenly

山では天気が急変することがあるから、気をつけな

さい。Watch out, the weather can change suddenly in the mountains.

天気が回復する the weather improves

天気が続く／もつ the weather is holding up; the good weather will last

なんとか明日まで天気がもってくれるといいのですが。I really hope the weather will hold until tomorrow.

天気に恵まれる be blessed with beautiful weather

今回の旅行は、天気に恵まれて楽しかった。We enjoyed the beautiful weather and the trip very much.

天気予報
weather
forecast

天気予報を聞く／見る check the weather forecast

天気予報はいつもテレビで見ている。I usually check the weather forecast on TV.

天気予報で…と言っている the weather forecast says ...

天気予報では、明日は雪になると言っています。The weather forecast says it will snow tomorrow.

天気予報がはずれる the weather forecast proves wrong

ありがたいことに天気予報がはずれて、雨は降らなかった。Fortunately the weather forecast proved wrong and it didn't rain.

天気予報が当たる the weather forecast proves right

日
sun

日が照る the sun shines

日が差し込む the sun shines/streams in

この部屋は午前中、よく日が差し込む。This room gets a lot of sunshine in the morning.

日が昇る［沈む］the sun rises [sets]

日が当たる get a lot of sunshine; be sunny

十分に日が当たるように、植物を窓際に移した。I moved the plants to the window so that they get enough sunshine.

日にさらされる be exposed to the sun

日に焼ける discolor from the sun; fade in the sunlight; get suntanned

その本の表紙は日に焼けていて、タイトルさえ読み

取れなかった。The cover of the book was discolored from the sun, so I couldn't even read the title.

日が暮れる it gets dark

　日が暮れないうちに、テントを立てなければ。We must put up the tent before it gets dark.

日が長く［短く］なる the days get longer [shorter]

　だいぶ日が短くなってきた。The days have gotten considerably shorter.

日が（西に）傾く the sun has begun to sink/set (in the west)

雪
snow

雪が降る it snows

　今日、この冬初めての雪が降った。Today it snowed for the first time this winter.

雪が降り出す／降り始める it begins snowing

雪が止む it stops snowing

雪が積もる the snow accumulates

　目が覚めたら、10センチも雪が積もっていた。I woke up to find the snow had accumulated to 10 centimeters.

雪に覆われる be covered with snow

　山頂付近は、すっぽりと雪に覆われている。The mountaintop is covered with snow.

雪に閉じ込められる be snowed in

　私の出身地の町では、冬の間雪に閉じ込められる。My hometown gets snowed in during the winter.

雪をかく shovel snow

雪が溶ける the snow melts/thaws

雪が多い have a lot of snow

雪が少ない have little snow

　今年は例年に比べて、ずいぶん雪が少ない。We have had much less snow than usual.

雪になる it will snow

　今夜は雪になりそうだ。It looks like we will have snow tonight.

雪に変わる turn to snow

お昼ごろに、雨が雪に変わった。The rain turned to snow around noon.

Post Office

きって
切手
stamp

切手を買う buy a stamp
　８０円の切手を１０枚、買ってきてもらえる？
Would you go and buy ten 80-yen stamps?
切手を貼る put a stamp on
　速達で送るのに、いくらの切手を貼ればいいか知っ
ていますか？ Do you know what the postage is for
express mail?
切手を貼り忘れる forget to put a stamp on
　しまった！　今投函したはがきに、切手を貼り忘れ
た！ Oh no! I forgot to put a stamp on the postcard I
just put in the mailbox!
切手をはがす remove a stamp; peel a stamp off
切手を売る［買う］sell [buy] a stamp
　コンビニでも切手を売っていますよ。Stamps are
also available at convenience stores.
切手を集める collect stamps
　父はここ２０年ほど、切手を集めています。My father
has collected stamps for the last 20 years.
（新しい／記念）切手が出る／発売される a (new/com-
memorative) stamp will go on sale

こづつみ
小包
package

（…を）小包にする make ... into a package (to send to
someone)
小包を出す send a package
小包を送る send a package
　アメリカに小包を送りたいのですが。I'd like to send
a package to the U.S.
小包で送る send something in a package
小包を受け取る receive a package
小包が届く receive a package; a package arrives
　京都の姉から小包が届いた。I received a package

from my sister in Kyoto.

小包が破損している a package is damaged when deliv-

ered; a package arrives damaged

手紙・はがき
letter, postcard

手紙を出す mail a letter

途中でこの手紙を出してもらえる？ Would you mail

this letter for me on the way?

手紙が届く receive a letter

手紙を受け取る／もらう receive/get a letter

英語を教えた生徒から、手紙をもらいました。I got

a letter from a student I taught English to.

手紙を書く write a letter

旅先で知り合った友人に、手紙を書いた。I wrote a

letter to a friend I met during the trip.

手紙を読む read a letter

人の手紙を読んじゃだめだよ。You shouldn't read

someone else's letter.

手紙を航空便／船便で送る send a letter by airmail/

sea mail

手紙を速達で送る send a letter by special delivery

郵便
mail

郵便を出す mail a letter

郵便が届く receive a letter

私あてに郵便は届いていませんか？ Is there any mail

for me?

郵便を受け取る receive a letter

郵便が来る the mail comes/arrives

うちにはふつう、午前１１時ごろ郵便がくる。Usu-

ally the mail comes to my place around 11 a.m.

郵便を配達する deliver mail

Bank

ＡＴＭ

ATM で（現金を）引き出す withdraw money from an

ATM

ATM で入金する deposit money through an ATM

ATMで送金する／振り込む transfer money through an ATM

銀行の窓口よりも、ATMで振り込むほうが手数料は安い。You'll be charged less commission if you transfer money through an ATM rather than asking to do so at a bank counter.

ATMで両替する change money through an ATM

ATMで下ろす withdraw money from an ATM

コンビニに寄ってATMで1万円下ろした。I stopped by at a convenience store and withdrew 10,000 yen from an ATM.

お金・現金
money, cash

（銀行に）お金を預ける deposit money (in a bank)

お金を引き出す withdraw money

カードを忘れてきたので、お金を引き出せない。I can't withdraw money because I forgot to bring my card.

お金を下ろす withdraw money

お金を貯める save money

日本中を旅行して回るために、お金を貯めています。I'm saving money so that I can travel around Japan.

お金を増やす increase money

お金を積み立てる put aside some money

クレジット（カード）
credit card

クレジットカードを使う use a credit card

クレジットカードは使えますか？ Do you accept credit cards?

クレジットで…を買う buy ... on credit

クレジットで新しいパソコンを買った。I bought a new computer on credit.

クレジット払いにする pay by credit card

クレジットカードで払う pay by credit card

公共料金の多くは、クレジットカードで払うことができます。Most utility bills can be paid by credit card.

口座
bank account

口座を開く［閉じる］open [close] a bank account

口座を持っている have a bank account

ほとんどの人は、複数の口座を持っている。Most people have more than one bank account.

口座を解約する close an account

もう使わなくなった口座を解約した。I closed the account I no longer use.

(…を) 口座引き落としにする have … paid directly from one's bank account

スポーツクラブの会費は、口座引き落としになっている。The membership fee for the sports club is paid directly from my bank account.

口座をつくる open an account

ミドリ銀行に、給与振込用の口座をつくった。I opened an account at Midori Bank to receive my salary.

口座を分ける open a separate account

(…を) 口座に振り込む transfer/pay … into the bank account

参加費は今月末までに、次の口座に振り込んでください。Please pay the fee to the account below by the end of this month.

口座に入金する deposit money into one's account

手数料
commission

手数料がかかる commission is charged

この銀行は、ATM での引き出しや入金には、手数料がかからない。This bank charges no commission for withdrawals and deposits made through an ATM.

手数料を払う pay commission

手数料が含まれる commission is included

この金額には、手数料は含まれていますか？ Is commission included in the price?

手数料が高い [安い] commission is high [low]

手数料が上がる [下がる] commission is raised [lowered]

そのサービスは手数料が下がって、利用しやすくなった。Now that the commission has been lowered, we can use the service more often.

手数料を取られる commission is charged

預金
savings

（銀行に）預金がある have money in one's bank account
今、預金が100万円ほどあります。I have about one million yen in my bank account now.
（銀行に）預金がない don't have money in one's bank account
預金を下ろす withdraw money from one's bank account
預金を引き出す withdraw money from one's bank account
預金を増やす increase money in one's bank account
この低金利では、預金を増やすのは難しい。It's difficult to increase money in the bank with such a low interest rate.

Shopping

お金
money

お金を払う pay money
お金を払うときになって、財布を忘れてきたことに気が付いた。I didn't realize that I had forgotten to bring my wallet until I was about to pay.
お金を渡す give money
お金が足りない be short of money
お金が足りなくて、最新型の掃除機は買えなかった。I didn't have enough money to buy the latest vacuum cleaner model.

お釣り
change

お釣りをもらう receive change
お釣りを間違える give the wrong amount of change
スーパーのレジで、お釣りを間違えられた。The cashier at the supermarket gave me the wrong amount of change.
お釣りがいらない／出ない give/pay the exact amount of money (so that there's no need for giving change)
バスに乗るときは、お釣りがいらないように小銭を準備するといい。When you ride on a bus, you should have small change so that you can pay the exact amount of the fare.

買い物
shopping

お釣りを渡す give change
買い物に行く go shopping
　日曜日にはよく渋谷に買い物に行きます。I often go shopping in Shibuya on Sundays.
買い物に出かける go out shopping
　ミキは買い物に出かけていて、留守です。Miki's not in. She's gone out shopping.
買い物から戻る come back from shopping
　買い物から戻るとすぐに、夕食の準備をした。I began preparing dinner as soon as I came back from shopping.
買い物を済ませる finish shopping
　クリスマスの買い物はもう済ませましたか？ Have you finished Christmas shopping yet?

価値
value

価値がある be valuable; be worth ...
　この絵は少なくとも５０万円の価値がある。This painting is worth at least half a million yen.
価値がない have no worth
価値が高い［低い］ be of great [little] value
価値が出る increase in value
　そのサインも、あと10年くらいたてば価値が出るかもしれない。That autograph might increase in value in about 10 years.
価値が上がる［下がる］ rise [drop/fall] in value

財布
wallet, purse

財布を持ち歩く carry one's wallet
　彼はいつも財布をズボンの尻ポケットに入れて持ち歩いている。He always carries his wallet in his back pocket.
財布をなくす lose one's wallet
　いつどこで財布をなくしたのか、見当がつかない。I have no idea when and where I lost my wallet.
財布を落とす lose one's wallet
　家から駅までの間で、財布を落としたに違いない。I must have dropped my wallet somewhere between home and the station.

財布を盗まれる have one's wallet stolen
電車の中で、財布を盗まれた。I had my wallet stolen in the train.

財布をすられる be pickpocketed

財布を拾う find someone's wallet

財布を取り出す take one's wallet out

商品
product, goods

商品が並ぶ goods are displayed
私が店に行ったときには、棚にはわずかな商品しか並んでいなかった。When I got to the store, there were only a few goods left on the shelf.

商品を仕入れる stock/buy products

商品を扱う deal in products; stock a product
何軒かの店を回ったが、どこもその商品を扱っていなかった。I went to several stores, but none of them had that item.

商品を売る sell products

商品を高く［安く］売っている sell products at high [low] prices

商品が揃っている have a wide variety of goods

スーパー・コンビニ
supermarket,
convenience
store

スーパーに行く go to a supermarket
週に1回スーパーに行って、1週間分の食料を買います。I go to a supermarket once a week and buy enough groceries for that week.

スーパーに（立ち）寄る drop by a supermarket
帰りにスーパーに寄って、牛乳を買ってきて。Will you get some milk at the supermarket on your way home?

スーパーで買い物（を）する shop at a supermarket; do shopping at a supermarket

スーパーが開く［閉まる］the supermarket opens [closes]
近所のスーパーは、朝9時に開く。The supermarket nearby opens at 9 a.m.

値段
price

値段が高い［安い］be high [low] priced; the price is high [low]
品質のいいものは、やはり値段が高い。High-quality

items are usually high priced as well.

値段が上がる［下がる］ the price goes up [down]

値段が上がり続ける［下がり続ける］ the price keeps going up [down]

ガソリンの値段が上がり続けている。Oil prices have kept going up.

値段をつける set a price

値段がつけられない be priceless

これらのアンティークは、値段がつけられないほど貴重だ。These antiques are priceless.

値段が表示されていない the price is not shown

値段がついていない don't have a price tag; the price has not been set

値段を確かめる check the price

物価
prices

物価が高い［安い］ prices are high [low]

ロンドンは物価が高い。Prices are high in London.

物価が上がる［下がる］ prices go up [down]

ここ1年でずいぶん物価が下がった。Prices have gone down considerably in the past year.

物価が安定する prices are stable

店
shop, store

店が開く［閉まる］ the store opens [closes]

いくつか部品を買おうと思ったら、店が閉まっていて買えなかった。I thought I would buy some parts, but when I went to the store it was closed, so I couldn't by them.

店に入る enter a store; go into a store

店を出る leave a store; go out of a store

店で買う／求める buy ... at a store

ペットを飼いたいなら、店で買う以外にも選択肢はある。If you want to have a pet, there are ways to get one other than buying at a pet shop.

店を見て回る look around in a store

友人に贈るプレゼントを探して、いろいろな店を見て回った。I looked around in various stores for a present to give to a friend of mine.

店（先）に並ぶ goods are displayed at (the front of) a store

レジ
cash register

レジに並ぶ stand in a checkout line
大勢の客がレジに並んでいた。 A lot of customers were standing in the checkout lines.

レジに進む go to the checkout (counter)

レジで精算する check out at the register

レジが混む there is a long line at the checkout counter
この時間帯は、いつもレジが混む。 There is always a long line at the checkout counter at this time of day.

レジを打つ operate a cash register

Restaurants

注文
order

注文する order; place an order
私たちは全員、今日のおすすめランチを注文した。 All of us ordered today's lunch special.

注文を取る take one's order

注文を取りに来る come to take one's order
若いウェイターが注文を取りに来た。 A young waiter came to take our orders.

注文を決める decide what to order

注文を受ける receive/get/accept an order

注文を取り消す cancel an order
デザートを頼んだのですが、食べられそうにありません。注文を取り消せますか。 I ordered a dessert, but I don't think I can eat it. Can I cancel it?

メニュー
menu

メニューをもらう ask for the menu
すみません、メニューをもらえますか? Excuse me, but may I have the menu please?

メニューを見る look at the menu
メニューを見ても、どんな料理なのかさっぱりわからなかった。 I looked at the menu, but had no idea what kind of food it was.

メニューを頼む ask for the menu

レストラン
restaurant

レストランを探す look for a restaurant

ホテルにチェックインした後、町に出てレストランを探した。After checking into the hotel, we went out and looked for a restaurant.

レストランを予約する reserve a table at a restaurant

今夜7時に、レストランを予約してあります。I've reserved a table at a restaurant at seven tonight.

レストランに入る go into a restaurant

レストランで夕食をとる have dinner at a restaurant

Cars & Commuting

ガソリン
gas(oline)

ガソリンを入れる put gas in

車にガソリンを入れないといけないから、少し早めに出ましょう。We need to put some gas in the car, so let's leave a bit early.

ガソリンが切れる run out of gas

ガソリンを食う consume a lot of gas

この車はガソリンを食うので、エコカーに買い替えるつもりだ。This car is such a gas guzzler, I'm going to buy an eco-car to replace it.

ガソリンを満タンにする fill it/her up

切符・乗車券
ticket

切符を買う buy a ticket

自動券売機で切符を買う方法がわかりません。I don't know how to buy a ticket in the ticket machine.

乗車券を求める buy a ticket

特急乗車券は、ホーム中程の券売機でお求めください。Please buy a limited express ticket from the ticket machine located in the middle of the platform.

切符をなくす lose one's ticket

彼は電車に乗ると、いつも切符をなくす。Every time he gets on a train, he loses his ticket.

切符を落とす lose one's ticket; drop one's ticket

切符を再発行してもらう have one's ticket reissued
切符を払い戻してもらう get a refund for a ticket
　出張がキャンセルになったので、切符を払い戻して

もらった。My business trip was canceled, so I got a

refund for the ticket.
乗車券を改める (an inspector) inspects one's ticket
切符を見せる show one's ticket

車
car

車を運転する drive a car
　免許は持っていますが、ふだんは車を運転しません。

I have a driver's license, but usually I don't drive a

car.
車で通勤する／通学する drive to work/school
　全社員のうち半分は、車で通勤しています。About

half of the whole staff come to work by car.
車に乗る get in a car
車に乗せてもらう be given a ride
車に同乗する share a car; car-pool
車が動かない the car won't start
車がエンストする the car stalls; the car engine gives

out
車を停める park a car; pull up a car
　車は駅の近くの駐車場に、停めてあります。I parked

my car in the parking lot by the station.
車を(月賦で)買う buy a car (on a monthly installment

plan)
車を借りる rent a car; borrow someone's car
車を(…に)ぶつける crash/bump one's car into ...
車を修理に出す have one's car repaired
車のタイヤがパンクする a car's tire goes flat

(座)席
seat

(座)席に座る sit in a seat; take a seat
(座)席をゆずる give (up) one's seat
　電車では、いつも高齢者に席をゆずるようにしてい

る。I often give up my seat to senior citizens.
(座)席を取る take a seat; make a seat reservation
席を取っておく keep/save one's seat

あなたの席を取っておきましたよ。I've saved a seat for you.

席が空いている a seat is open/unoccupied

席を代わる switch seats

窓際に座っていた人が、席を代わってくれた。The person sitting at the window gave me his seat.

席を交換する change/exchange seats

席を立つ stand up from one's seat; leave one's seat

渋滞
traffic jam

渋滞に巻き込まれる get caught in a traffic jam

渋滞に巻き込まれてしまい、予定より1時間も遅れて目的地に着いた。We got caught in a traffic jam and arrived at our destination an hour late.

渋滞を避ける avoid a traffic jam

渋滞を避けるために別の道を選んだが、たいして変わらなかった。I chose another route so as to avoid the traffic jam, but it didn't really work.

渋滞する be backed up

渋滞で動きが取れない be stuck in a traffic jam

渋滞にはまる be stuck in a traffic jam

渋滞にはまって、6時間も車の中に閉じ込められた。We were in the car for six hours stuck in a traffic jam.

定期(券)・回数券
commuter pass,
commuter coupon
ticket

定期を買う buy a commuter pass

定期を買うために並んでいるのですか？ Are you waiting to buy a commuter pass?

定期を使う use a commuter pass

定期を忘れる forget one's commuter pass

定期を忘れたので、切符を買わなければならない。I forgot my commuter pass, so I have to buy a ticket.

定期をなくす lose one's commuter pass

新しく買ったばかりだったのに、不注意にも定期をなくしてしまった。I had just bought a new commuter pass, but I carelessly lost it.

定期を落とす lose one's commuter pass

定期が切れる one's commuter pass expires

あと1週間で定期が切れる。My commuter pass will

expire in a week.

列・行列
line

列ができる a line forms

その店の前には、客の長い列ができていた。There was a long line of customers in front of the shop.

列を作る form a line

列に並ぶ line up; get in line; join a line

列に並んでまで、そのドーナツを買いたいとは思わない。I don't feel like lining up just to buy those donuts.

列に割り込む cut/break into the line

中年のおばさん二人組が、平気で列に割り込んできた。Two middle-aged women shamelessly cut into the line.

列を無視する ignore the line

列の最後尾につく join the end of the line

Hospital & Pharmacist

医者
doctor

医者に診てもらう (go and) see a doctor

明日も熱が下がらないようなら、医者に診てもらったほうがいいよ。You should go see a doctor if your temperature stays high tomorrow.

医者に相談する consult a doctor

アレルギー体質なので、その薬を飲む前に医者に相談した。I consulted a doctor before taking the medicine because I have an allergic constitution.

医者に…を止められる be advised to stop ... by a doctor

医者にかかる see/consult a doctor

私は持病のぜんそくで、医者にかかっています。I'm seeing a doctor about my usual asthma.

医者を呼ぶ call a doctor

医者を呼びましょうか？ Shall I call a doctor?

インフルエンザ
flu

インフルエンザにかかる catch the flu

インフルエンザにかかってしまったかもしれない。

I might have caught the flu.

インフルエンザになる catch the flu

インフルエンザが治る get over the flu

インフルエンザが流行する the flu spreads
今年の冬は、インフルエンザが大流行すると報道されている。The media says the flu will be prevalent this winter.

インフルエンザを予防する prevent catching the flu
インフルエンザを予防する最も効果的な方法は、うがいと手洗いだ。The most effective way to prevent catching the flu is by gargling and washing your hands.

インフルエンザがうつる get/catch the flu

お見舞い
visit
(to a sick person)

お見舞いに行く visit/go and see (a sick person in the hospital)
昨日、足を骨折して入院している友人のお見舞いに行った。Yesterday I visited a friend who is in the hospital with a broken leg.

お見舞いを断る refuse someone's visits

お見舞いを言う express one's concern

お見舞いを渡す give a (get-well) present
彼女にお見舞い(の品)を渡すよう、頼まれました。
She asked me to give you this present.

お見舞いの花を届ける send flowers/have flowers delivered (to a sick person in the hospital)

風邪
cold

風邪をひく catch/get a cold
私はめったに風邪をひきません。I seldom catch colds.

風邪をひいている have a cold
今、私の周りのたくさんの人が風邪をひいています。A lot of people around me have a cold now.

風邪をひきやすい be susceptible to colds

風邪が治る get over a cold
今年の風邪はしつこくて、なかなか治らない。This year's colds are really stubborn and hard to shake off.

風邪をこじらせる make one's cold worse

　風邪をこじらせるといけないから、もう１日休みを
取ったら？ Why don't you take another day off in
order not to make your cold worse?

風邪がぶり返す one's cold comes back

風邪がうつる catch/get a cold

風邪がはやる a cold spreads/goes around

　風邪がはやっているので、気をつけてください。Take
good care of yourself since a cold is going around.

風邪を予防する prevent catching a cold

花粉症
hay fever,
pollen allergy

花粉症だ have an allergy to pollen; suffer from hay fever

家族全員が花粉症です。Everyone in my family suf-
fers from hay fever.

花粉症になる become allergic to pollen

　どうやら今年から花粉症になったようだ。It looks
like I developed an allergy to pollen this year.

花粉症が悪化する one's allergy to pollen gets worse

けが
injury

けがの手当をする treat an injury

　救急隊の一人が、けがの手当をしてくれた。A mem-
ber of the rescue team treated my injury.

けがの手当を受ける have one's injury treated

けがで入院する be hospitalized with an injury

けがが治る an injury heals

　完全にけがが治るまで、運動は禁止です。You must
not do exercise until the injury heals.

健康
health

健康にいい［悪い］be good [bad] for the health

　オリーブ油は健康にいい。Olive oil is good for the
health.

健康に気をつける take care of one's health

　１度病気をしてから、健康に気をつけるようになっ
た。After suffering from an illness, I began to take
better care of my health.

健康に恵まれる enjoy good health

健康を保つ keep fit; stay healthy

　彼は若さと健康を保つために、毎朝ジョギングをして

いる。He jogs every morning in order to stay young and healthy.

健康を損なう damage/ruin one's health

頭痛
headache

頭痛がする have a headache

ゆうべから頭痛がします。I've had a headache since last night.

(偏)頭痛がひどい have a bad headache; have a migraine

頭痛が治まる one's headache eases/goes away

この薬を飲んで少ししたら、頭痛は治まった。I took this medicine, and after a while my headache was gone.

頭痛持ちだ suffer chronic headaches

せき
cough

せきをする cough; give a cough

せきをしているけど、風邪ですか？ You are coughing. Do you have a cold?

せきが出る cough

せきがひどい have a bad/heavy cough

せきが止まらない one's cough won't go away

夜になるとせきが止まらなくなって、とても苦しい。My cough won't go away at night and is very painful.

体調
physical
condition

体調がいい be in good condition/shape

毎朝のジョギングを始めたら、最近とても体調がいい。Recently I got in very good shape after I started jogging every morning.

体調が悪い be in poor condition/shape

今日は体調が悪いので、パーティーはパスします。I don't feel well today, so I'll skip the party.

体調を整える get into shape

来週富士山に登るので、体調を整えておかなければ。I'm going to climb Mt. Fuji next week, so I have to get into shape.

体調を崩す fall sick; ruin oneself

彼は体調を崩して、先月から休職しています。He fell sick and has been on sick leave since last month.

体調を取り戻す get back into shape

体力
strength

体力を消耗する use up all one's strength

１時間ボクシングの練習をして、すっかり体力を消耗してしまった。After practicing boxing for an hour, I was totally exhausted.

体力が回復する regain one's strength

体力を蓄える save one's strength

明日は忙しくなりそうだから、体力を蓄えておこう。It looks like I'll have a busy day tomorrow, so I think I'll save my strength.

体力をつける gain strength

体力がある［ない］be physically strong [weak]

体力があるので、一日や二日徹夜しても全く平気です。I'm pretty strong, so staying up for a night or two will be no problem at all.

血
blood

血が出る bleed

彼は自転車で転んで、ひざから血が出ていた。He fell off his bike and was bleeding from a wound on his knee.

血が流れる bleed; blood runs/flows

はっと気がついたら、額から血が流れていた。I suddenly noticed I was bleeding from my forehead.

血が噴き出す blood gushes out

血が止まる bleeding stops

傷口をしばらくの間押さえておくと、血は止まります。If you press the wound for a while, the bleeding will stop.

血を止める stop the bleeding

血がつく get bloodstains

鼻血が出て、シャツに血がついてしまった。I had a nosebleed and got bloodstains on my shirt.

血がにじむ blood smears

血を吐く vomit blood

血が固まらない blood doesn't clot/coagulate

血を採る take blood; take a blood sample

血が足りない be short of blood

熱
fever,
temperature

熱がある have a fever

顔が赤いけど、熱があるんじゃない？ Your face looks flushed. Do you have a fever?

熱が出る run/have a fever

高い熱が出たときは、インフルエンザの可能性が高い。 If you have a high fever, you probably have caught the flu.

熱を出す run/have a fever

熱が高い have a high fever

熱をはかる take/check one's temperature

熱をはかったら、３７．８度ありました。 I took my temperature and the thermometer read 37.8 degrees.

熱が下がる［上がる］ one's fever goes down [up]

翌日になってようやく熱が下がってきた。 My fever finally began to go down the next day.

熱に浮かされる be delirious with a fever

洟・鼻水・鼻
runny nose

洟／鼻水が出る have a runny nose

この季節は、毎日のように洟が出て止まらない。 I have a runny nose almost every day in this season.

洟をかむ blow one's nose

洟／鼻水をすする sniffle

待合室のあちこちから、洟をすする音が聞こえてきた。 I heard people sniffling everywhere in the waiting room.

鼻が詰まる one's nose gets stuffed up

病院
hospital

病院に行く go to a hospital

この５年間、病院に行っていません。 I haven't been to a hospital for the last five years.

病院に通う go to a hospital on a regular basis

アトピーの治療のため、病院に通っています。 I go to the hospital on a regular basis to receive treatment for a skin allergy.

病院で手当を受ける receive medical treatment at a hospital

病院で待たされる be forced to wait for a long time at

a hospital

病院はとても混んでいて、1時間以上待たされた。

The hospital was crowded and I had to wait for more than an hour.

病院で薬を処方してもらう ask for a prescription

病気
illness

病気になる fall ill; get sick

そんな不摂生を続けていたら、病気になるよ。You will fall ill if you keep living such an unhealthy life.

病気が治る get well; get over one's illness

病気から快復する get over one's illness

病気が悪化する one's illness worsens

彼は持病が悪化して、先週入院した。His chronic disease worsened and he was hospitalized last week.

病気で入院する be hospitalized with (a) disease

病気で寝込む be sick in bed

病気で衰弱する become weak because of one's illness

病気を治す cure (a) disease

きちんと病気を治して、また仕事に復帰したい。I want to cure my disease completely and get back to work.

病気を予防する prevent (a) disease

病気に効く work on illness

これらのハーブは、いろいろな病気に効くとされています。These herbs are said to work on various illnesses.

病気をしたことがない have never fallen ill

病気をうつす give one's disease (to someone else)

病気で亡くなる die of (a) disease

私の父は78歳のとき、病気で亡くなりました。My father died of a disease at age 78.

薬局・薬剤師
pharmacy,
pharmacist

薬局で薬を買う buy medicine at a pharmacy

薬局で薬をもらう get/receive medicine at a pharmacy

薬局が併設されている a dispensary is provided

大きな病院には、たいてい薬局が併設されています。Most big hospitals have a dispensary.

薬剤師に相談する consult a pharmacist

Dentist & Optometrist

コンタクト(レンズ)
contact lens

コンタクトをする／している wear contacts
　ふだんは眼鏡ですが、運動するときはコンタクトを
しています。I usually wear glasses, but I switch to contacts when exercising.

コンタクトを入れる put in one's contacts
　初めてコンタクトを入れたときは、なかなかうま
く入れられなかった。When I first tried to put in my contacts, it wasn't easy.

コンタクトをつける wear contacts

コンタクトをはめる put in one's contacts

コンタクトをはずす take out one's contacts
　コンタクトをはずすのを忘れて寝てしまい、翌朝は
目が痛くて大変だった。I had forgotten to take out my contacts before going to sleep, so my eyes really hurt the next morning.

コンタクトをなくす lose one's contacts
　私はしょっちゅうコンタクトをなくすので、使い捨
てのものに変えた。I often lose my contacts, so I've begun using disposable ones.

コンタクトを割る break one's contacts

歯石
tartar

歯石がつく tartar accumulates
　いくら毎日歯磨きをしても、歯石がつくのは避けら
れない。Tartar accumulation is unavoidable even if you brush your teeth every day.

歯石ができる tartar accumulates

歯石を取る remove tartar
　1年に1回、歯医者で歯石を取ってもらうことにし
ています。I make it a rule to have tartar removed from my teeth at the dentist once a year.

視力
eyesight

視力を測ってもらう have one's eyesight checked

先日、眼科で視力を測ってもらった。I had my eyesight checked at the ophthalmologist the other day.

視力の検査をする／受ける have one's eyesight checked

視力が落ちる one's eyesight gets worse/poorer

目を使う仕事を始めてから、視力が落ちた。My eyesight got worse since I started a job that strains the eyes.

視力が回復する one's eyesight gets better

レーシック手術を受けて、劇的に視力が回復した。After LASIK eye surgery, my eyesight improved dramatically.

視力を矯正する correct one's eyesight

視力を失う lose one's eyesight

彼女は小さいころに、病気で視力を失った。She lost her eyesight due to a disease when she was small.

歯
teeth

歯を抜く have a (bad) tooth pulled

来週、虫歯を1本抜くことになった。I'm going to have a bad tooth pulled out next week.

歯を白くする whiten one's teeth

歯がいい［悪い］ have good [bad] teeth

歯が痛い／痛む have a toothache

歯が痛くて、ゆうべは一睡もできなかった。Because of a toothache, I didn't get a wink of sleep last night.

歯が抜ける one's tooth comes out

歯がぐらぐらする one's tooth is loose

歯にしみる make one's tooth hurt

アイスのように冷たいものを食べると、歯にしみる。Cold stuff like ice cream makes my tooth hurt.

歯が欠ける one's tooth breaks

歯にはさまる get stuck between one's teeth

トウモロコシの皮が歯にはさまってしまった。Some corn got stuck between my teeth.

歯の矯正をする have one's teeth straightened

アメリカでは、小さいときに歯の矯正をするのが、一

般的だ。In the United States, people usually have their teeth straightened at a young age.

歯を治す／治療する treat/fix one's (bad) teeth

歯が生える cut teeth

歯が抜ける a tooth comes out

歯が抜け替わる a tooth comes out and will be replaced by a permanent tooth

歯医者
dentist

歯医者を予約する make an appointment with the dentist

残念ですが、明日の午後は歯医者を予約しています。 Unfortunately I have an appointment with the dentist tomorrow afternoon.

歯医者に診てもらう consult/go to see a dentist

歯医者に行く go to the dentist('s)

子どものころは、歯医者に行くのがいやでたまらなかった。 I just hated going to the dentist when I was a child.

虫歯
cavity,
tooth decay

虫歯になる get a cavity

甘い物を食べると虫歯になるというのは、必ずしも正しくない。 It's not necessarily true that cavities are caused by eating sweet stuff.

虫歯がある have a cavity

虫歯があると、そこから菌に感染することがある。 You might get infected by some viruses through a cavity.

虫歯ができる get a cavity

虫歯を治療する treat a decayed/bad tooth

虫歯を抜く pull out a decayed/bad tooth

虫歯が痛い／痛む a decayed tooth hurts

虫歯を予防する prevent tooth decay

虫歯を予防するには、毎食後の歯磨きが大切だ。 It's important to brush your teeth after each meal to prevent tooth decay.

め
目
eye

目がいい have good eyesight; one's eyesight is good
　目がいい人たちが、うらやましい。I envy people
who have good eyesight.
目が悪い have poor eyesight; one's eyesight is poor
目が疲れる one's eyes get sore
　パソコンの画面をずっと見ていると、目が疲れる。
My eyes get sore when I look at the computer screen
for a long time.
目が腫れる one's eyes get swollen
　朝起きたら、目が少し腫れていた。When I got up
in the morning, my eyes were a bit swollen.
目がかゆい one's eyes feel itchy
　スギ花粉の飛ぶ季節になると、目がかゆくてたまら
ない。My eyes feel really itchy when the cedar pollen starts getting blown by the wind.
目が悪くなる one's (eye)sight gets worse
　そんな暗い所で本を読んでいると、目が悪くなるよ。
Your sight will get worse if you read books in such a
dim place.
目を悪くする damage one's eyesight
目がかすむ one's vision is blurred
　最近、夕方になると目がかすむ。Recently my vision
gets blurred in the evening.
目にできものができる get an eye rash
目にゴミが入る get something in one's eye
目が赤い／充血している one's eyes are bloodshot
涙目になる one's eyes become moist (with tears)

めがね
眼鏡
glasses

眼鏡をかける wear glasses; put on one's glasses
　写真の真ん中にいる、眼鏡をかけた人が私の兄です。
The guy with the glasses in the middle of the photo
is my brother.
眼鏡の度が合わない the glasses are not right for ...
　そんなに目が疲れるというのは、眼鏡の度が合っていな
いのかもしれない。Maybe you get sore eyes because
your glasses are not right for your eyesight.

眼鏡のレンズがはずれる a lens comes off its frame
眼鏡をはずす／とる take off one's glasses
　眼鏡をとると、まるで別人のようだね。You look totally different without your glasses.
眼鏡を買う buy glasses
眼鏡をつくる／あつらえる have lenses made

Hair & Beauty

髪(の毛)
hair

髪を切る／カットする have one's hair cut
　私は1か月に1回、髪を切ります。I have my hair cut once a month.
髪にパーマをかける have one's hair permed; get a perm
　気分転換に髪にパーマをかけた。I got a perm for a change.
髪を染める dye one's hair
　最近では、髪を染めるのがごく当たり前になってきた。Dyeing your hair has become very popular these days.
髪をセットする have one's hair set

床屋
barbershop

床屋に行く go to the barber('s)
床屋で散髪する have one's hair cut at the barber
　私は美容院よりも、床屋で散髪するほうが好きだ。I prefer having my hair cut at a barber rather than a beauty parlor.
床屋でひげをそってもらう have one's face shaved at the barber

ネイル(サロン)
nail salon

ネイルサロンに行く go to a nail salon
　どのくらいの割合で、ネイルサロンに行きますか？How often do you go to a nail salon?
ネイルをする have one's nails (professionally) done
　明日は友達の結婚パーティーなので、ネイルをした。I had my nails done because I'm going to a

friend's wedding party tomorrow.

ネイルを塗る have one's nails manicured

ネイルを付ける put on artificial nails

ネイルを付けた状態で、料理をしたり洗い物をしたりするのは難しい。 It's rather difficult to cook or do the dishes with artificial nails.

ネイルを落とす remove one's nail polish

美容院
beauty salon

美容院に行く go to a beauty parlor

美容院を予約する make an appointment with a beautician/hairdresser

来週水曜日に、美容院を予約した。 I made an appointment with my hairdresser for next Wednesday.

美容院に予約を入れる make an appointment with a beautician/hairdresser

美容院でセットする have one's hair set at a beauty parlor

パーティーの前に、美容院でセットしてもらうつもりです。 I'll have my hair set at the beauty parlor before the party.

美容院でカットしてもらう have one's hair cut at the beauty parlor

美容院で髪を染めてもらう have one's hair dyed at the beauty parlor

Troubles, Dangers & Annoyances

空き巣
breaking into a house (while the residents are away)

空き巣に入られる one's house is broken into while one is out

私の住んでいるアパートの隣の部屋が、空き巣に入られた。 The apartment next to mine was broken into while the neighbor was out.

空き巣が多い many thefts occur when people are not at home

このあたりは空き巣が多い。 There are a lot of thefts

in this area when residents are out.

空き巣を防ぐ prevent thefts while one is out

アクシデント・事故
accident

アクシデントが起こる an accident happens

アクシデントに見舞われる have an accident

今年に入ってから、様々なアクシデントに見舞われています。 I've had various accidents this year.

事故を起こす cause an accident

(交通)事故にあう get in an accident/a traffic accident

事故に巻き込まれる be involved in an accident

(爆発)事故が発生する an explosion occurs

危険
danger

危険にさらされる be exposed to danger

これらの動物は、絶滅の危険にさらされています。 These animals are in danger of extinction.

危険が伴う involve danger

ほとんどの手術には、ある程度の危険が伴うものだ。 Any surgery involves a certain amount of risk.

危険を避ける avoid danger

危険を逃れる escape danger

危険を察知する sense danger

人間には本来、危険を察知する力が備わっている。 Humans are naturally equipped with the ability to sense danger.

危険を冒す run a risk

彼は、自分の仕事を失う危険を冒して、私を助けてくれた。 He helped me despite running the risk of losing his job.

危険をかえりみない do not think of one's own safety

その店員は危険をかえりみず、強盗と格闘した。 The shop clerk fought with the robber, not thinking of his own safety.

危険が転がっている danger is everywhere

警察
police

警察に届ける report to the police

道で財布を拾ったので、警察に届けた。 I found someone's wallet on the street, so I brought it to the police.

警察に通報する notify the police

警察に知らせる notify the police

　何か変わったことがあったら、すぐに警察に知らせてください。If you notice anything unusual, please notify the police immediately.

警察を呼ぶ call the police

　隣の部屋の騒音があまりにひどかったので、警察に通報した。The noise from the next door was so bad that I called the police.

警察沙汰になる get the police involved

　彼は一度酔っ払いとけんかして、警察沙汰になったことがある。He once got into trouble with the police after picking a fight with a drunkard.

警察に助けを求める ask the police for help

警察に出頭する turn oneself in

（犯人を）警察に突き出す turn in a criminal to the police

警察の手が回る be searched/investigated by the police

煙
smoke

煙が出る smoke comes out

　電子レンジから煙が出ているよ！There's smoke coming out of the microwave!

煙が立ち込める be thick with smoke

　ホールにはあっという間に煙が立ち込めたそうだ。They say the hall was instantly filled with smoke.

煙に巻かれる be overcome by smoke

　その火事では、煙に巻かれて二人の客が亡くなった。Two customers died in the fire.

煙が立ち上る smoke rises up

煙を吸う breathe in smoke

煙にむせる choke on smoke

煙で目が痛い smoke stings one's eyes

けんか
fight

けんかをする have a fight/quarrel

　子どものころは、しょっちゅう兄とけんかをしたものだ。I would often fight with my brother when we were young.

けんかになる get into a fight/quarrel

意見が合わないときは、いつも私が折れるので、あまりけんかにならない。We hardly get into fights since I always give in when we disagree.

けんかに巻き込まれる get involved in a fight
君たち二人のけんかに巻き込まれたくない。I don't want to get involved in the fight between you two.

けんかを止める stop a fight

けんかの仲裁をする mediate a fight

けんかを売る／ふっかける pick a fight (with a person)

けんかを買う take up a challenge to fight
彼は売られたけんかは買う人だ。If someone challenges him to a fight, he always takes it up.

交番
police station

交番に駆け込む run to a police station
誰かに後をつけられているような気がして、思わず交番に駆け込んだ。I felt that someone was stalking me, so I ran to the police station in spite of myself.

交番で(道を)尋ねる／聞く ask for directions at a police station
すみません、(その場所は)わかりません。あそこの交番で聞いてみてください。Sorry, I don't know the place. Please ask at the police station over there.

交番に…を届ける take ... to a police station

困難・トラブル
difficulty

困難を乗り越える get over difficulties
そのピアニストは努力することで、いくつもの困難を乗り越えてきた。The pianist got over many difficulties through his own efforts.

困難をやり過ごす let hardships go by

困難に陥る get into difficulties
今、人生で最大の困難に陥っています。I've gotten into my biggest difficulty ever.

困難に打ち勝つ overcome/get over difficulties

困難に見舞われる be struck by hardship
彼女はどんな困難に見舞われようと、決してくじけなかった。She never gave up no matter what obstacle got in her way.

困難に直面する face difficulties

彼は経済的に大変な困難に直面している。He is now facing a serious financial problem.

困難に立ち向かう face a difficulty

困難に耐える bear/put up with hardships

彼らは戦争中、多くの困難に耐えてきた。They put up with many hardships during the war.

詐欺
fraud

詐欺にあう be swindled

その人は詐欺にあって、大金を騙し取られてしまった。He was swindled out of a large sum of money.

詐欺を働く commit fraud

その容疑者は違法な株の売買で、詐欺を働いたとされている。The suspect is said to have committed fraud by illegally trading stocks.

詐欺に注意する watch out for fraud

詐欺が増えている cases of fraud are increasing

詐欺が横行している fraud is rampant

詐欺に引っかかる fall for a scam

借金
debt

借金がある have debts; owe a person ...

私は彼に100万円の借金がある。I owe him one million yen.

借金を返す pay (back) one's debt

借金を抱えている be in debt

彼は銀行に対して、3千万円の借金を抱えている。He is 30 million yen in debt to the bank.

借金を完済する pay off one's debt; clear one's debt

借金を完済するのに、3年かかった。It took me three years to pay off my debt.

借金を踏み倒す avoid paying one's debts

その夫婦は借金を踏み倒して逃げた。The couple ran away without paying their debt.

借金を申し込む ask a person to lend one money

人口
population

人口が多い［少ない］have a large [small] population

人口が増える［減る］increase [decrease] in population

その市では、ここ5年間で20％人口が増えた。

The city increased in population by 20 percent over the last five years.

人口が集中する be densely populated

オーストラリアでは、沿岸地域に人口が集中している。Coastal areas are densely populated in Australia.

人口が倍増する population doubles

真相
truth

真相を知る know the truth

その事件の真相を知る人は、もはやこの世にいない。The people who know the truth about that incident are no longer alive.

真相を突き止める find out the truth

真相が明らかになる the truth emerges/comes out

犯人がつかまって、ようやく真相が明らかになった。

The criminal was caught and the truth finally came out.

生活
life

生活が苦しい be badly off

今は多くの人が、生活が苦しいと感じている。Many people feel that they are badly off now.

生活が楽になる be better off

生活がかかっている have to support oneself/one's family

生活を始める start a life

私たちは横浜に引っ越して、新しい生活を始めました。We moved to Yokohama and started a new life.

生活に困る have a hard time making a living

その男は生活に困って、コンビニで盗みを働いた。

Because the man had a hard time making a living, he shoplifted at a convenience store.

(…での)生活になじむ get used to life in ...

私はなかなか新しい生活になじめなかった。I had a hard time getting used to my new life.

生活を営む lead a life

彼は長野の山奥で、自給自足の生活を営んでいま

す。He is leading a self-sufficient life deep in the mountains in Nagano.

生活(習慣)が変わる one's life/lifestyle changes

騒音
noise

騒音に悩まされる be annoyed by noise

この部屋に越してきてから、ずっと騒音に悩まされている。I've been annoyed by noise ever since I moved into this apartment.

騒音がひどい the noise is terrible

騒音を注意する warn ... about the noise

アパートの上の階の住人に騒音を注意した。I warned the tenants on the upper floor about the noise.

騒音に文句を言う complain about the noise

騒動
disturbance

騒動が起きる trouble occurs

ゴミ出しをめぐって、近隣の住人たちの間で騒動が起きた。Trouble occurred among my neighbors over the issue of putting out trash.

騒動を鎮める put down a disturbance

騒動が収まる a disturbance settles down

騒動を(引き)起こす make/cause a disturbance

彼がこの騒動を引き起こした張本人だ。He is the one who caused the trouble.

治安
order, security

治安がいい be safe to live in

一般に、日本は治安がいいとされている。Generally speaking, Japan is considered to be a safe country to live in.

治安が悪い be unsafe to live in

治安が悪化する become less safe

その地域は最近、急速に治安が悪化している。That area is rapidly becoming less safe these days.

治安が回復する restore order

その国の治安が回復するのに、まだかなり時間がかかるだろう。It will take a fairly long time for that country to restore order.

治安を維持する maintain/keep order

泥棒・すり
thief,
pickpocket

泥棒が入る a thief breaks in
友人のアパートに先週、泥棒が入った。A thief broke into my friend's apartment last week.
泥棒をつかまえる catch a thief
泥棒を追いかける chase a thief
泥棒を取り逃がす fail to catch a thief; let a thief get away
店主はあと少しのところまで追いつめたが、結局泥棒を取り逃がした。The shop owner was close to catching the thief, but he failed in the end.
すりに財布を抜かれる／盗られる one's wallet is stolen by a pickpocket

火
fire

火が出る a fire starts
その居酒屋の厨房から火が出て、あっという間に燃え広がった。A fire started in the kitchen of the *izakaya* restaurant and immediately spread.
火が燃え上がる a fire blazes
火がつく something catches fire
昨日の雨で薪が湿っているので、なかなか火がつかない。The wood is wet from yesterday's rain, so it doesn't catch fire easily.
火をつける light a fire; set ... on fire
ろうそくに火をつけてください。Please light the candles.
火が消える a fire dies
花火をした後は、火が完全に消えているかどうか必ず確かめること。Make sure the fire is completely out after doing fireworks.
火を消す extinguish/put out a fire
火を吹き消す blow out a flame
火が回る a fire spreads
火を消し止める put out a fire
消防隊、1時間後にようやく火を消し止めた。An hour later, the firefighters finally put out the fire.
火が風で煽られる a fire is fanned by the wind
火が燃え移る a fire spreads (to ...)

被害
damage

被害にあう suffer damage

その手の詐欺の被害にあっているのは、ほとんどが高齢者だ。Senior citizens are the main victims of that kind of scam.

被害をこうむる suffer damage

被害を受ける suffer damage

被害を届ける report the damage

被害をもたらす cause/do damage

先月の台風は、中国地方に大きな被害をもたらした。Last month's typhoon caused extensive damage to the Chugoku region.

被害を最小限に食い止める keep the damage to a minimum

すぐにクレジットカードを止める手続きを取ったので、被害は最小限に食い止められた。I kept the damage to a minimum because I quickly made my credit card invalid.

水
water

水が漏れる water leaks

天井から水が漏れています。Water is leaking from the ceiling.

水があふれる water overflows; water runs over

地下の水道管が破裂して、道路に水があふれた。The underground water pipe burst and water ran all over the road.

水が引く water subsides

あふれた水が引くまで、ほぼ1日かかった。It took about a day until the floodwaters subsided.

水が出ない water doesn't come out (of the tap)

水が止まる the water supply is stopped

水につかる be soaked in water

水が(家に)入ってくる one's house is flooded above the floor

問題
problem

問題が起こる trouble occurs/emerges/comes up

私の留守中に何か問題が起こったら、この番号に電話してください。Call this number if any trouble comes up while I'm away.

問題を起こす cause trouble

彼は何か問題を起こして、会社を首になったという
うわさだ。There's a rumor that he caused some
trouble and got fired.

問題に直面する face a problem

問題を解決する solve a problem

その問題を解決するには、プロの弁護士に相談した
ほうがいい。You should ask for professional advice
from a lawyer in order to solve that problem.

問題になる become a problem

問題にならない be unimportant; be inconsequential

その程度の失敗は、全然問題にならない。Such a mistake doesn't matter at all.

問題だ be a problem; matter

私が誰からその話を聞いたかは、問題ではない。It
doesn't matter who told me the news.

問題に取り組む tackle a problem

リスク
risk

リスクを伴う carry a risk

その会社に投資するのは、かなりのリスクを伴う。
Investing in that company carries a lot of risk.

リスクを背負う take risk

それなりのリスクを背負う覚悟は、できていますか?
Are you prepared to take some risks?

リスクが大きい be risky

それほどよく知らない人と一緒に事業を始めるの
は、あまりにもリスクが大きい。It's too risky to start
a business with someone you don't know well.

リスクを小さくする reduce risk

リスクを避ける avoid risks

Payment & Paperwork

アパート
apartment

アパートを借りる rent an apartment
私は日本人の友人からアパートを借りています。I rent an apartment from a Japanese friend of mine.

アパートに住む live in an apartment

アパートに引っ越す move into an apartment
住み慣れた家を出て、小さなアパートに引っ越した。I left my old house and moved into a small apartment.

アパートを引き払う move out of one's apartment
先週彼を訪ねたが、すでにアパートを引き払った後だった。I went to visit him last week, but he had already moved out of his apartment.

アパートを探す look for an apartment
もっと職場に近いところで、アパートを探すことにした。I decided to look for an apartment closer to the office.

アパートを変わる change apartments

契約(書)
contract

契約(書)を交わす exchange contracts

契約を結ぶ sign a contract
その選手は、アーセナルと契約を結んだ。The player is signed with Arsenal.

契約が成立する a contract comes together

契約を更新する renew one's contract
この契約は、毎年自動的に更新される。This contract is renewed automatically every year.

契約が切れる／満了する a contract expires
この部屋の賃貸契約は、来月切れる。The lease on this apartment expires next month.

契約を延長する extend a contract

契約を破棄する cancel a contract
彼は一方的に契約を破棄されたとして、その会社を訴えるつもりだ。He is going to press charges against the company for unilateral cancelation of the contract.

契約違反をする breach/violate a contract

契約を守る fulfill a contract

光熱費
utility bills

光熱費を払う pay utility bills

ふだんは、コンビニで光熱費を払っています。I usually pay my utility bills at convenience stores.

光熱費を口座引き落としにする have utilities paid directly from one's bank account

光熱費が上がる［下がる］fuel and lighting expenses go up [down]

石油の値上がりの影響で、来月から光熱費が上がる。Due to higher oil prices, the fuel and lighting rate will be raised next month.

市役所・区役所
municipal office

(市)役所に転入届［転出届］を出す submit a change-of-address notice to the municipal office

(市)役所で住民登録する register as a resident at the municipal office

おとといこの町に引っ越してきて、今日、市役所で住民登録した。I moved into this town the day before yesterday and registered as a resident today.

(市)役所で住民票をとる have one's resident card issued at the municipal office

(市)役所で手続きをする go through procedures at the municipal office

税金
tax

税金を払う pay taxes

税金を納める pay taxes

税金がかかる a tax is imposed (on ...)

たばこには高い税金がかかっている。Tobacco is heavily taxed.

税金がかからない be tax-free

宝くじの当せん金には、税金はかかりません。A prize won in a lottery is tax-exempt.

税金が上がる［下がる］tax is raised [cut/reduced]

税金を滞納する be in arrears with one's taxes

税金に持っていかれる go to taxes; be collected as tax

その俳優は稼いだ金額の 6 割近くを、税金に持っ

ていかれると言った。The actor said that almost 60 percent of his earnings went to taxes.

税金を取られる be taxed

税金が返ってくる some taxes are refunded

来月までに確定申告をすれば、いくらか税金が返ってきます。If you file your final income tax return by next month, you'll receive a tax refund.

税金が引かれる tax is deducted

日本での居住期間が1年未満の場合は、20％の税金が引かれます。Twenty percent of the tax will be deducted if you have been in Japan less than one year.

宅配便
delivery service

宅配便がくる a package comes by home delivery service

今日の午後2時から4時の間に、宅配便がくる予定だ。I'm going to receive a package by home delivery service sometime between 2 and 4 p.m.

宅配便が届く a package arrives by home delivery service

宅配便を受け取る receive a package by home delivery service

宅配便で送る send a package by home delivery service

旅行先から、荷物を宅配便で送った。I had my stuff delivered by home delivery service from where I was staying.

宅配便を扱う deal in home delivery service

電気・ガス・水道
electricity, gas, water supply

電気代の請求がくる receive an electricity bill

電気代を払う pay an electricity bill

電気代を滞納する be in arrears with one's electricity bills

電気を止められる electricity is turned off

一定の期間、電気代を滞納していると、電気を止められる。If you fail to pay the bills for a certain amount of time, the electricity will be turned off.

ビザ
visa

ビザを取る／取得する obtain a visa

就労ビザを取るためには、いろいろな条件を満た

していなければならない。You have to meet various qualifications in order to obtain a work visa.

ビザを申請する apply for a visa

中国への入国ビザを申請しました。I applied for an entry visa to China.

ビザを発給する issue a visa

ビザを書き換える renew one's visa

来月、ビザを書き換えなければならない。I have to renew my visa next month.

ビザが切れる one's visa expires

しまった！　ビザが切れてた！ Oh no! My visa has expired!

ビザが下りる［下りない］a visa is issued [not issued]

ビザがなかなか下りなくて、困っている。I'm troubled by the length of time it is taking for my visa to be issued.

ビザがいる［いらない］a visa is required [not required]

ビザを免除する exempt a visa

日本人は 9 0 日未満の短期滞在であれば、アメリカのビザは免除される。Visa-exempt entry to the U.S. is applicable to Japanese for short stays within 90 days.

ビザを偽造する forge a visa

費用
expense, cost

費用を切り詰める cut down on expenses/costs

あらゆる面で、できるだけ費用を切り詰めるようにしないといけない。We are supposed to try to cut down on every cost.

費用を見積もる estimate the expense/cost

その旅行の費用を一人当たり 7 5,000 円と見積もった。I estimated the cost of the trip at 75,000 yen per person.

費用を負担する pay the expenses

ありがたいことに、かかった費用はすべて会社が負担してくれた。Fortunately, all the expenses incurred were paid by the company.

費用を折半する split the cost
フェンスの修理にかかる費用は折半することになった。We agreed to split the cost of fixing the fence.
費用がかかる cost
費用を惜しむ spare expenses
愛犬の治療には、いくらかかっても費用は惜しまない。I'd spare no expenses for my dog's treatment no matter how much the cost.

部屋
room

部屋を借りる rent a room/an apartment
部屋を貸す rent out a room
部屋を使う use a room
東京にいる間は、この部屋を自由に使ってくれていいよ。You can use this room freely while you are in Tokyo.
部屋を探す look for an apartment
このあたりで部屋を探しているのですが、何かいい物件はありますか？ I'm looking for an apartment around here. Could you recommend one?
部屋をシェアする share an apartment
私は中国人一人、カナダ人二人と部屋をシェアしている。I share the apartment with a Chinese and two Canadians.

保険・保険料
insurance

保険に入る／加入する buy insurance
車に乗るなら、保険には必ず入っておくべきだ。If you drive a car, you should definitely have insurance.
私は 5,000 万円の生命保険に入っています。I have insured myself for 50 million yen.
保険を解約する cancel one's insurance
保険をかける insure ...
この家には、2,000 万円の火災保険をかけている。I have insured my house against fire for 20 million yen.
保険に勧誘する sell insurance
保険がある［ない］be insured [uninsured]
保険料を払う pay an insurance premium
保険料を納める pay an insurance premium

免許（証）
license,
driver's license

免許を取る　get a license

アメリカ人の多くは、高校生のときに運転免許を取ります。Most Americans get a driver's license when they are in high school.

免許を持っている　have a license

私は調理師の免許を持っています。I have a chef's certificate.

免許（証）を見せる　show one's license

免許を更新する　renew one's license

免許を更新するのに、わざわざ遠くの警察署まで行かなければなりません。I have to go all the way to a distant police station to renew my license.

家賃
rent

家賃を払う　pay the rent

家賃の交渉をする　negotiate the rent

不動産屋の人が大家と家賃の交渉をしてくれた。The real estate agent negotiated with the landlord about the rent.

家賃を滞納する／家賃が滞る　be in arrears with one's rent

彼は2か月分の家賃を滞納したまま、突然行方をくらましました。He suddenly disappeared without paying two months' rent.

家賃を（銀行で）振り込む　pay the rent into a bank account

家賃が上がる　one's rent is raised

PEOPLE

Looks

足・脚
foot, leg

脚が長い have long legs
そのモデルは脚が長くてすらりとしている。The fashion model has long slender legs.
脚が短い have short legs
足が大きい have big feet
彼は足が大きいから、この靴は入らないだろう。He has big feet, so these shoes won't fit him.
足が小さい have small feet
彼は背丈の割に、足が小さいほうだ。He has rather small feet for his height.
脚が細い have slender legs
脚が太い have fat/thick/big legs
彼女は脚が太いことを気にしている。She doesn't like her fat legs.
足が不自由だ have difficulty walking

ウエスト
waist

ウエストが細い have a slender/slim waist
私もあなたみたいにウエストが細かったらなあ。I wish I had a slender waist like you.
ウエストが太い have a large/thick waist
ウエストが締まっている have a slender/slim waist
毎日の運動の成果が出ているのか、だんだんウエストが締まってきた。My waist is getting smaller, maybe because I've been working out every day.
ウエストがくびれている have a slender/slim waist

顔
face

顔が大きい have a big face
顔が小さい have a small face
顔が丸い have a round face

顔が長い have an oval face; have a long face

　肖像画を見ると、その武将はずいぶん顔が長かった
ようだ。From the portrait, it looks like the samurai
general had quite a long face.

顔が面長だ have an oval face

(可愛い／醜い)顔をしている have a pretty/an ugly face

髪(の毛)
hair

髪が長い have long hair

髪が伸びる one's hair grows

　髪が伸びてきたから、そろそろ散髪に行かなくちゃ。

My hair has grown long. It's about time to get a hair-
cut.

髪が短い have short hair

髪を短くする cut one's hair short

　夏向きに髪を短くしてもらいたいのです。I'd like
to have my hair cut short for summer.

髪が多い have thick hair

　私は髪が多いほうだ。I have rather thick hair.

髪が少ない have thin hair

髪が硬い have coarse hair

　この髪型は、髪が硬いとうまくいかない。This hairstyle is not good for coarse hair.

髪が柔らかい have soft hair

(黒い／茶色い)髪をしている have black/brown hair

髪を染めている have one's hair dyed; one's hair is dyed

髪を伸ばしている wear one's hair long

髪を三つ編み／お下げ／ポニーテールにしている wear
one's hair in braids/pigtails/a ponytail

髪をアップにしている wear one's hair up

しわ
wrinkle

(顔に)しわがある[ない] have wrinkles [no wrinkles]
(on one's face)

しわが多い have a lot of wrinkles

しわが少ない have few wrinkles

しわが増える get more wrinkles

　私の姉はここ数年で、ずいぶんしわが増えてきた。

My sister has gotten a lot more wrinkles over the last

few years.

しわができる get wrinkles

しわを寄せる wrinkle up (one's brow, etc.)

スタイル
figure

スタイルがいい have a nice figure; have a nice body/physique

そのアイドルは、抜群にスタイルがいい。The pop idol has a great body.

スタイルが崩れる lose one's figure

スタイルを保つ keep one's figure

スタイルを保つ秘訣は何ですか? What's your secret to keeping your figure?

背
height

背が高い be tall

ケイトは私が思っていたより、背が高かった。Kate was taller than I had expected.

背が低い be short

背が伸びる grow

弟は昨年の春から、ずいぶん背が伸びました。My brother has grown a lot since last spring.

胸
breast, chest

胸が大きい have large breasts; be full-chested

胸が小さい have small breasts; be flat-chested

胸が垂れている have sagging breasts

目
eye

目が大きい have large eyes

兄は父に似て、目が大きい。My brother has large eyes like our father.

目が小さい have small eyes

目が二重／一重だ have double-fold/single-fold eyelids

彼女は目が一重だということを気にしている。She is not happy with her single-fold eyelids.

目が垂れている have drooping eyes

目が吊り上がっている have upturned eyes

目が黒い／青い have dark/blue eyes

目が赤くなっている one's eyes are bloodshot

目が澄んでいる have clear eyes

目がくぼんでいる have sunken/deep-set eyes

指
<ruby>指<rt>ゆび</rt></ruby>
finger

<ruby>指<rt>ゆび</rt></ruby>が<ruby>長<rt>なが</rt></ruby>い have long fingers

この<ruby>子<rt>こ</rt></ruby>はとても<ruby>指<rt>ゆび</rt></ruby>が<ruby>長<rt>なが</rt></ruby>いから、ピアニストになるといいよ。 He should become a pianist since he has such long fingers.

<ruby>指<rt>ゆび</rt></ruby>が<ruby>短<rt>みじか</rt></ruby>い have short fingers

<ruby>指<rt>ゆび</rt></ruby>が<ruby>細<rt>ほそ</rt></ruby>い have slender fingers

<ruby>指<rt>ゆび</rt></ruby>が<ruby>太<rt>ふと</rt></ruby>い have thick fingers

Traits

頭
<ruby>頭<rt>あたま</rt></ruby>
brains

<ruby>頭<rt>あたま</rt></ruby>がいい be smart/clever; be intelligent

なるほどね。<ruby>君<rt>きみ</rt></ruby>は<ruby>頭<rt>あたま</rt></ruby>がいいよ。 I see. You're so smart.

<ruby>頭<rt>あたま</rt></ruby>が<ruby>悪<rt>わる</rt></ruby>い be stupid; have no brains

<ruby>頭<rt>あたま</rt></ruby>が<ruby>切<rt>き</rt></ruby>れる be sharp/clever/smart

<ruby>今度<rt>こんど</rt></ruby>の<ruby>部長<rt>ぶちょう</rt></ruby>は、<ruby>非常<rt>ひじょう</rt></ruby>に<ruby>頭<rt>あたま</rt></ruby>が<ruby>切<rt>き</rt></ruby>れると<ruby>評判<rt>ひょうばん</rt></ruby>だ。 Our new manager has a reputation for being very clever.

<ruby>頭<rt>あたま</rt></ruby>が<ruby>冴<rt>さ</rt></ruby>えている be sharp

<ruby>頭<rt>あたま</rt></ruby>が<ruby>鈍<rt>にぶ</rt></ruby>い be dense/slows

<ruby>頭<rt>あたま</rt></ruby>がおかしい be crazy; have a screw loose

腕
<ruby>腕<rt>うで</rt></ruby>
skills, talent

<ruby>腕<rt>うで</rt></ruby>が<ruby>立<rt>た</rt></ruby>つ one's talent shows

<ruby>料理人<rt>りょうりにん</rt></ruby>として<ruby>腕<rt>うで</rt></ruby>が<ruby>立<rt>た</rt></ruby>つようになるまでには、<ruby>何年<rt>なんねん</rt></ruby>もの<ruby>修業<rt>しゅぎょう</rt></ruby>が<ruby>必要<rt>ひつよう</rt></ruby>だ。 You will need many years of training before your talent as a cook will show.

<ruby>腕<rt>うで</rt></ruby>に<ruby>覚<rt>おぼ</rt></ruby>えがある be confident in one's skills; be talented/skillful

ビデオの<ruby>撮影<rt>さつえい</rt></ruby>なら、<ruby>腕<rt>うで</rt></ruby>に<ruby>覚<rt>おぼ</rt></ruby>えがあります。 I'm confident in my skills at filming videos.

<ruby>腕<rt>うで</rt></ruby>がいい／<ruby>腕<rt>うで</rt></ruby>のいい be skillful/competent

<ruby>腕<rt>うで</rt></ruby>のいい<ruby>歯医者<rt>はいしゃ</rt></ruby>を<ruby>私<rt>わたし</rt></ruby>に<ruby>紹介<rt>しょうかい</rt></ruby>してくれませんか? Will you recommend a good dentist to me?

(…する)<ruby>腕<rt>うで</rt></ruby>がある have the skills to do ...

勘
<ruby>勘<rt>かん</rt></ruby>
hunch

<ruby>勘<rt>かん</rt></ruby>がいい［<ruby>悪<rt>わる</rt></ruby>い］ be quick [slow] to catch on

<ruby>勘<rt>かん</rt></ruby>が<ruby>鋭<rt>するど</rt></ruby>い be sharp; have a good nose for ...

<ruby>彼<rt>かれ</rt></ruby>は<ruby>勘<rt>かん</rt></ruby>が<ruby>鋭<rt>するど</rt></ruby>いから、そんなうそは<ruby>通<rt>とお</rt></ruby>らないよ。 He is

sharp, so such a lie won't work with him.

勘が鈍い be slow to catch on

　君は相変わらず勘が鈍いなあ。You are slow to catch on as usual.

勘が当たる［外れる］one's hunch is right [wrong]

　君の勘が当たったようだ。やっぱりあいつはぺてん師だったよ。It looks like your hunch was right. That guy turned out to be a swindler.

勘が働く one's intuition tells one something

　その日に限って、私は崩落したトンネルを通らなかったのです。何かがおかしいという勘が働いたとしか思えません。On that particular day, I didn't go through the tunnel that collapsed. I cannot but think my intuition told me something was wrong.

声 voice

声が高い have a high-pitched voice

　彼の声は高くて、神経にさわる。His voice is high-pitched and gets on my nerves.

声が低い have a low-pitched voice

　彼女は女性にしては、かなり声が低い。She has a very low-pitched voice for a woman.

声がきれいだ have a beautiful voice

　ユカは合唱部でいちばん声がきれいだ。Yuka has the most beautiful voice in our chorus club.

声がハスキーだ have a husky voice

声がいい have a good voice

声が渋い have a seasoned voice

声がよく通る have a voice that carries well

信仰 faith, belief

信仰を持つ have faith (in ...)

信仰を捨てる abandon one's faith (in ...)

信仰心が篤い be religious/devout

　この地方の人々は、一般に信仰心が篤い。People in this area are generally religious.

信念 belief, principles

信念を持つ have one's beliefs; have convictions

信念を曲げる abandon one's beliefs/principles

　私は信念を曲げてまで、その地位を得たいとは思いま

せん。I don't want to achieve the position by abandoning my principles.

信念を貫く stick to one's principles

我々が何と言おうと、彼は自分の信念を貫くだろう。

He'll stick to his principles no matter what we tell him.

知恵
brains

知恵をしぼる rack one's brains

どの店も売り上げを伸ばそうと知恵をしぼっている。

All the store owners are racking their brains for ways to increase sales.

知恵が働く be smart

そんな奇抜なアイディアを思いつくなんて、よく知恵が働くものだね。How smart you are to come up with such an extraordinary idea!

悪知恵が働く use cunning/craftiness

知恵を働かせる use one's brains/head

知恵が浮かぶ hit on a good idea

入浴中にいい知恵が浮かんだ。I hit on a good idea while taking a bath.

知恵が回る be shrewd/clever

甥はまだ5歳だというのに、よく知恵が回る。My nephew is only five, but he is really clever.

知恵遅れだ be mentally retarded

知識
knowledge

知識が豊富だ have a good knowledge (of ...)

彼は、日本の伝統工芸に関する知識が豊富だ。He has a good knowledge of Japanese traditional handicrafts.

知識が乏しい have little knowledge (of ...)

この本は、科学の知識が乏しい人のために、やさしく書かれている。This book is written in easy terms for people who have little scientific knowledge.

知識がある know about ...; be knowledgeable (about ...)

コンピューターに関する知識はありますか。Are you knowledgeable about computers?

判断
judgment

判断を下す judge; make a judgment; make a decision

その問題について、早まった判断を下すべきではあ

りません。You should not make a hasty judgment on the matter.

判断に迷う have trouble making a decision; cannot make a prompt decision

判断に迷ったら、いつでも相談してください。You can consult me anytime you have trouble making a decision.

判断がつく［つかない］can [cannot] decide; can [cannot] make a decision

彼の仕事の申し出を受けるべきかどうか、判断がつかない。I can't decide whether I should accept his job offer.

理解
understanding

理解が速い［遅い］be quick [slow] at understanding; pick things up quickly [slowly]

彼は物事の理解が速いので、どんな仕事も任せられる。He picks things up quickly, so I can trust him with any kind of job.

理解がある understand; show understanding

私たちの会社は子育てに理解があり、女性にとっては働きやすい。Our company understands the challenges of raising children, so it is a good place for women to work.

理解がない don't understand/appreciate

リサイクルの重要性に、理解がない人が多すぎる。Too many people don't understand the importance of recycling.

Personality

頭
mind

頭が低い be humble

頭の回転が速い［遅い］have a quick [slow] mind; be quick [slow]-witted

彼は信じられないほど頭の回転が速い。私にはとてもついて行けない。He is incredibly quick-witted. I can hardly keep up with him.

頭が柔らかい be flexible (in one's way of thinking)

彼は、あなたが考えるより、はるかに頭が柔らかい人だ。He is far more flexible than you think.

頭が固い be stubborn

父は頭が固いので、説得するのにいつも苦労する。

My father is stubborn, and it's hard to persuade him of anything.

頭が古い be old-fashioned in one's way of thinking; be too conservative

こんな意見をブログに載せるなんて、彼はよほど頭が古い人なんだろう。He must be really old-fashioned to post such opinions on his blog.

気
temper

気が大きい be generous

彼は酒を飲むと、時々気が大きくなる。He sometimes becomes generous when he drinks alcohol.

気が小さい be timid

その話し方から、彼は気が小さいとわかる。You can tell he is timid by the way he speaks.

気が短い be short[quick]-tempered; have a short temper

彼女は気が短いのが、唯一の欠点だ。Her only fault is that she is short-tempered.

気が長い be patient

気が強い be strong-minded

リカはいかにも気が強そうな顔をしている。You can tell Rika is strong-minded by her looks.

気が弱い be timid

彼は一見気が弱そうだが、はっきりと自分の意見を言う。He looks timid, but actually he expresses his opinions frankly.

気が多い be capricious; be whimsical

気がきく be considerate

あなたは本当に気がきかない人ね。雨が降り出したら、洗濯物くらい取り込んでよ。You are so clueless. You should have at least taken in the laundry when it started raining.

気が荒い have a violent temper

気がいい／気のいい be good-natured

気が置けない／気の置けない be close; one can feel at ease (with ...)

気の置けない友人たちを呼んで、パーティーをした。
I had a party with some close friends of mine.

口 mouth

口がうまい have a smooth/slick tongue; be a smooth talker

彼は口がうまいから、あまり信用するな。He is a smooth talker, so don't believe everything he says.

口が軽い have a big mouth

口がかたい can keep a secret

彼に相談してみたらどう？ 彼は口がかたいよ。Why don't you ask him for advice? He can keep a secret.

口が悪い have a sharp tongue

口が悪いのは、いつものことでね。彼のことを勘弁してやってください。He just has a sharp tongue. That's the way he is. Please forgive him.

尻 bottom, buttocks

尻が重い be slow to take action

尻が軽い be thoughtless; be careless

尻に敷かれている be henpecked

遅かれ早かれ、彼は尻に敷かれた夫の典型になるだろう。Sooner or later, he will be a typical henpecked husband.

尻が長い one overstays one's welcome

中には尻の長い人もいる。Some people just don't know when to leave.

性格 character, nature

性格がいい［悪い］ have a good [bad] nature

彼女は性格がいいので、みんなから愛されている。She is loved by everybody because of her good nature.

性格が違う have a different character; be different in character

トムとジェイクは双子の兄弟だが、性格はずいぶん違

う。Tom and Jake are twin brothers, but they have quite different characters.

性格が明るい［暗い］have a cheerful [gloomy] personality

性格が明るいと、人間関係を築くうえで大いにプラスになると思います。I believe a cheerful personality is a great advantage in building good relationships with people.

性格が合う get along (with ...); agree (with ...)

新しい上司とは、どうも性格が合わない。I just can't get along with my new boss.

手
hand

手が早い be fast (with ...); be quick to use violence

手が付けられない be out of control

彼女はいったん怒り出すと、手が付けられなくなる。She often gets carried away once she gets angry.

手に余る be too much (for ...); be too hard/difficult (for ...); cannot handle

この機械の操作は難しくて、私の手に余る。This machine is too difficult for me to operate.

手に負えない be too much (for ...); cannot handle

あの少年はやんちゃ過ぎて、私の手に負えない。That boy is too naughty for me to handle.

鼻
nose

鼻が高い be proud

鼻にかける be proud (of ...); boast (about/of ...)

あいつはいつも学歴を鼻にかけるから嫌いだ。I hate that guy because he always boasts about his academic background.

鼻の下が長い drool over (a woman)

彼は金髪美女を前にして、鼻の下が長くなっていた。He was drooling over the blond beauty.

鼻がきく have a (good) nose (for ...)

彼女はおいしいレストランには、鼻がきく。She has a good nose for restaurants.

鼻につく get on one's nerves

あの人はいつも親切そうにしているのが鼻につく。

He always tries to come across as Mr. Nice Guy, and
it gets on my nerves.

目
eye

鼻もちならない be intolerable

目がきく have a keen/sharp eye (for ...)

私の兄は趣味で絵を描くので、絵画には目がきく。

My brother paints pictures as a hobby, so he has a
sharp eye for paintings.

目がない have a weakness (for ...)

彼女は甘いもの、特にチョコレートには目がない。

She has a weakness for sweet things, especially
chocolate.

(物を見る)目がある have an eye (for ...)

目が高い have a good eye

この本の価値がわかるとは、なかなかお目が高いで
すね。The fact that you appreciate this book shows
you are a good judge of quality.

目が肥えている have a critical eye (for ...)

我が社の新製品は、目が肥えた日本の消費者を満足さ
せるでしょう。Our new products will satisfy Japan's
discriminating consumers.

目でものを言う convey one's thoughts with one's eyes

Feelings

頭
head, mind

頭にくる get angry

彼からのメールを読んで猛烈に頭にきたので、返信
をしなかった。His e-mail made me really angry, so
I didn't reply to it.

頭が痛い give one a headache

来週の就職面接試験のことを考えると、頭が痛い。

Thinking about next week's job interview gives me
a headache.

頭が上がらない cannot oppose/stand up to ...

彼はいつも偉そうなことを言っているくせに、部長に

は頭が上がらない。He always talks big, but he can-not stand up to the manager.

（…で）頭がいっぱいだ be preoccupied (with ...)
彼女はその難局をどう乗り切るかで、頭がいっぱいだ。She's preoccupied with how to get through the difficult situation.

頭がこんがらがる get confused
彼の説明を聞いているうちに、私はなんだか頭がこんがらがってきた。I was getting confused listening to his explanation.

頭から離れない can't get ... out of one's mind
別れた彼女のことが頭から離れない。I can't get my ex-girlfriend out of my mind.

頭が変になりそうだ something is driving one crazy; feel like one is losing one's mind

怒り
anger

怒りがこみ上げる anger wells up (in a person)
怒りがこみ上げてきて、思わず拳を握りしめた。I felt anger welling up in me and clenched my fists unconsciously.

怒りに震える shake/tremble with anger
彼女は怒りに震えながら、「出て行って！」と男に言った。Trembling with anger, she said to the man, "Get out of here!"

怒りに満ちている be full of anger

怒りが爆発する explode with rage
彼の身勝手な態度に、彼女の怒りは今にも爆発しそうだった。She was simmering with rage at his selfish attitude.

怒りをぶちまける vent one's anger (on ...)
彼はオフィスに戻ってくるなり、同僚たちに怒りをぶちまけた。He vented his anger on his colleagues as soon as he came back to the office.

怒りに駆られる be driven by anger (to do); anger spurs a person on
彼は怒りに駆られて、目の前のゴミ箱を蹴飛ばした。

Spurred by anger, he kicked the trash can in front of him.

怒りを覚える feel anger; anger rises up (in a person)

今回の理不尽な判決に、私たちは皆怒りを覚えています。We all feel great anger at this unfair judgment.

怒りを抑える suppress one's anger

怒りを抑えられなくなり、私は彼の顔を殴りつけた。I couldn't suppress my anger any longer and punched him in the face.

怒りを鎮める soothe a person's anger

怒りを買う make a person angry; arouse a person's anger

今さら言い訳しても遅いよ。彼女の怒りを買うだけさ。It's too late to make excuses. It will only make her angry.

印象
impression

印象を与える impress; make an impression (on ...)

あなたの礼儀正しい話し方は、面接官にいい印象を与えるでしょう。Your polite way of speaking will make a favorable impression on the interviewer.

印象を受ける get an impression

そのチームはよくまとまっているという印象を受けました。I got the impression that the team was well organized.

印象をもつ have an impression

彼は非常に人情に厚い人だという印象をもっています。He has impressed me as being very warm-hearted.

印象が薄い be unimpressive

彼女は信頼の置ける社員だが、やや印象が薄い。She is a reliable worker, but she is somewhat unimpressive.

印象に残る be impressive

その映画でいちばん印象に残ったシーンはどこですか？ Which scene of the movie impressed you the most?

顔
face

顔から火が出る blush/flush with embarrassment

生徒の一人から間違いを指摘されて、顔から火が出

る思いでした。I blushed with embarrassment when one of my students pointed out my mistake.

顔に書いてある be written on a person's face

　隠そうとしてもだめだよ。ちゃんと顔に書いてあるよ。It's no use trying to keep it secret from me. It's written on your face.

(感情が)顔に出る (one's feelings) show on one's face

顔が赤くなる one's face blushes; one turns bright red

悲^{かな}しみ
grief, sorrow

悲しみに耐える bear grief

悲しみに包まれる be filled with grief

　その英雄の死に、国中が深い悲しみに包まれた。The whole country was filled with deep sorrow over the death of the hero.

悲しみに打ちひしがれる be shattered/overwhelmed with grief

　その夫婦は娘を亡くした悲しみに、打ちひしがれていた。The couple were shattered with grief over their daughter's death.

悲しみに沈む be deep in sorrow

　彼は親友を事故でなくして、悲しみに沈んでいる。He is deep in sorrow because his best friend was killed in the accident.

感情^{かんじょう}
feeling, emotion

感情を込める put a person's emotions (into ...)

　教師は生徒たちに、感情を込めて歌うように言った。The teacher told her students to sing with more feeling.

感情を抑える control one's feelings

感情を害する hurt a person's feelings; be offended

　私の言ったことで感情を害されたのなら、謝ります。I apologize if my words offended you.

感情を抱く have feelings (about ...)

　誰でも故郷には、特別な感情を抱いているものだ。Everyone has special feelings about their hometown.

感情に流される be swayed by one's feelings

　彼の弱点は、感情に流されやすいということだ。His weak point is that he is easily swayed by his feelings.

感情に訴える appeal to a person's emotions

演説には政策に関する具体的な話はほとんどなく、主に有権者の感情に訴えるものだった。The speech contained few specifics about policy, and was mainly an appeal to voters' emotions.

感情が高ぶる get excited

カナダに出発する前の晩、彼女は感情が高ぶってよく眠れなかった。The night before leaving for Canada, she was excited and couldn't sleep well.

感情を表す show one's feelings

彼は人前では、めったに感情を表すことがない。He seldom shows his feelings in front of other people.

気
nature, temper, mind

気が合う get along well (with ...)

カズオは私の同僚だが、どうも気が合わない。Kazuo is my colleague, but I just don't get along well with him.

気が重い feel depressed

今後の住宅ローン返済のことを考えると、気が重い。The thought of repaying my mortgage makes me feel depressed.

気が気でない be really worried (about ...)

私たちの乗った飛行機に、今にも雷が落ちるのではないかと気が気でなかった。I was really worried that our plane might be struck by lightning at any moment.

気が進まない be unwilling to do; be reluctant to do

彼女を待たずに先に行くのは、気が進まなかった。I was reluctant to go ahead without her.

気がとがめる feel guilty

彼との約束を破ってしまったことで、非常に気がとがめた。I felt really guilty about breaking my promise to him.

気が引ける feel uncomfortable

この問題について上司に掛け合うのは、少々気が引ける。I feel a little uncomfortable negotiating with my boss about this matter.

気がめいる feel depressed
こう長いこと雨が続くと、気がめいってしまう。Such long spells of rain make me feel depressed.

気が変わる change one's mind
彼女をドライブに誘おうと思っていたが、気が変わった。I was going to ask her to go for a drive, but I changed my mind.

気になる be concerned/worried; be interested
彼女は昨日具合が悪そうだったので、気になっていたんです。I was worried about her because she looked sick yesterday.
彼は受付の女の子のことが気になるようだ。He seems interested in the girl at the reception desk.

気が抜ける feel relieved; feel relief

**気分
mood**

気分がいい［悪い］be in a good [bad] mood
くじでテレビが当たったので、今日は気分がいい。I feel great today because I won a TV in a lottery.

気分が晴れる be cheered up; be refreshed
湖畔でも散歩すれば、気分が晴れるよ。Taking a walk around the lake will cheer you up.

気分がふさぐ get depressed
彼は最近、気分がふさいでいるようだね。どうしたんだろう。He looks depressed these days. What's the matter with him?

気分が盛り上がる get excited; be cheered up
コンサートが進むうちに、私たちはますます気分が盛り上がってきた。As the concert went on, we got more and more excited.

気分を害する be offended
彼の不用意な発言に、彼女は気分を害した様子だった。She seemed offended by his careless remark.

気分がすっきりする feel refreshed
シャワーを浴びたら、気分がすっきりした。I felt refreshed after taking a shower.

気分が最悪だ feel terrible/horrible

二日酔いで今朝は気分が最悪だ。I'm hung over and feel terrible this morning.

気分が最高だ feel great

気分が爽快だ／さわやかだ feel refreshed

心
heart, mind

心が痛む one's heart aches

飢餓のどん底にある人々のことを思うと、心が痛む。

My heart aches for the people living in extreme hunger.

心が弾む one's heart jumps/leaps

彼女からメールをもらうと、心が弾みます。My heart jumps with joy when I get e-mail from her.

心にもない don't really mean something

彼は心にもないことを言って、彼女を怒らせた。

He made her angry by saying something he didn't really mean.

心を打つ move; impress; be moving/impressive

その映画のラストシーンには、見るたびに心を打たれる。The last scene of that film moves me every time I see it.

心を奪われる be fascinated/captivated

心を動かされる be moved/affected/touched

ショック
shock

ショックを受ける be shocked

親友が列車事故で亡くなったと聞いて、彼はショックを受けた。He was shocked to hear that his best friend was killed in the train accident.

ショックを与える shock

その有名歌手の逮捕のニュースは、彼の熱心なファンにショックを与えた。The news that the famous singer was arrested shocked his adoring fans.

ショックから立ち直る get over a shock; recover from a shock

彼女はその事件のショックから、立ち直りかけている。She is getting over the shock of the incident.

神経
nerves

神経が疲れる be hard on one's nerves; be nerve-wracking

あの傲慢な部長の下で仕事をするのは、さぞ神経が疲れるでしょう。It must be hard on your nerves to work under that arrogant manager.

神経が高ぶる become nervous

そのピッチャーは登板を前にして、神経が高ぶっているようだ。The pitcher looks nervous as he prepares to take the mound.

神経にさわる get on one's nerves

あの騒々しい音楽は、神経にさわる。That noisy music gets on my nerves.

神経が参る crack; snap; have a nervous breakdown

厳しい訓練で、彼は神経が参ってしまうのではないかと心配だ。I'm worried that the hard training might make him crack.

神経をすり減らす wear out one's nerves; fray one's nerves

劣悪な労働環境の中で、神経をすり減らしている人は多い。Many people are worn out due to poor working conditions.

神経をとがらせている be nervous (about ...)

政府は首相退陣を求める世論の高まりに、神経をとがらせている。The government is getting nervous about growing public demand for the prime minister's resignation.

神経を集中させる focus one's concentration (on ...)

彼は目の前のモニターの画面に、神経を集中させた。He focused his concentration on the monitor in front of him.

神経を逆なでする rub a person the wrong way

彼の配慮に欠けた発言は、被害者の神経を逆なでした。His indiscreet remark rubbed the victims the wrong way.

神経を使う worry (about ...)

私のことで、あれこれ神経を使っていただかなくても大丈夫ですよ。You don't have to worry so much about me.

精神
mind

精神が不安定だ be mentally unstable

ストレスがたまると、精神が不安定になりやすい。

Too much stress can make people mentally unstable.

精神を集中させる concentrate one's attention (on ...)

バッターは投手に精神を集中させて打席に立った。

The batter stepped to the plate, concentrating his attention on the pitcher.

精神に異常をきたす become mentally ill; go out of one's mind

精神を鍛える discipline one's mind; develop mental discipline

精神を鍛えるために、兄は剣道を始めた。My brother has started practicing kendo to develop mental discipline.

腹
stomach

腹が立つ get angry

あまり腹が立ったので、私は電話をガチャンと切ってしまった。I got so angry that I slammed down the phone.

腹にすえかねる can't stand/bear

彼の傍若無人の振る舞いは、腹にすえかねる。I can't stand his insolent behavior.

腹の虫がおさまらない be not satisfied (with ...)

彼を1発殴ったくらいでは、とても腹の虫がおさまらない。There's no way I will be satisfied just giving him a punch.

身
body

身が縮む freeze; cringe

闇にうごめく人影を見て、恐怖で身が縮む思いだった。I froze when I saw a figure moving in the dark.

身につまされる sympathize (with ...) deeply

被害者が私の娘と同じ年だと知って、身につまされる思いだった。I felt deep sympathy when I learned the victim was the same age as my daughter.

身にしみる be grateful; keenly realize; have something hit home

友人の大切さが身にしみてわかった。It hit home how precious my friends are.

胸
heart

胸が痛む feel sorry; one's heart breaks

彼女のメールを読んで、胸が痛んだ。My heart broke when I read her e-mail.

胸がいっぱいになる one's heart is full of ...; one's heart fills with ...

支援者からたくさんの励ましの手紙をもらい、彼は感謝で胸がいっぱいになった。His heart filled with gratitude when he received the many encouraging letters from his supporters.

胸が騒ぐ／胸騒ぎがする feel uneasy

胸がつまる get a lump in one's throat

病院のベッドに横たわる母親を見て、彼女は胸がつまった。She got a lump in her throat when she saw her mother lying in bed in the hospital.

胸がはりさける one's heart bursts

事故現場を訪れるたびに、私は胸がはりさけそうです。My heart almost bursts whenever I visit the scene of the accident.

胸にしみる hit home

胸にこたえる have something hit home; something strikes one

喜び
joy, delight,
pleasure

喜びに包まれる be filled with joy/delight

彼女が金メダルを獲得したというニュースに、国中が大きな喜びに包まれた。The news that she won a gold medal filled the whole nation with great joy.

喜びにあふれる be filled with joy/delight

喜びをかみしめる fully appreciate the joy of something

試合から 1 週間たって、ようやく優勝の喜びをかみしめています。A week has passed since the game, and finally I've come to fully appreciate the joy of winning.

喜びを味わう experience joy/pleasure

喜びがこみ上げる feel joy rising (in ...)
そのメールを読むうちに、喜びがこみ上げてきた。
I felt joy rising in me as I read the e-mail.
喜びに沸く be jubilant (over ...); resound with joy
地元のチームが優勝して、町はいま喜びに沸いている。The town was jubilant over its team's winning the championship.

Thought & Behavior

アイディア
idea

アイディアが浮かぶ an idea occurs to one; an idea comes to mind
散歩をしている最中に、彼は新製品のアイディアが頭に浮かんだ。An idea for a new product came to him while he was taking a walk.
アイディアを思いつく hit on an idea; come up with an idea
彼らは、電気を節約するための斬新なアイディアを、いくつか思いついた。They came up with some fresh ideas for saving electricity.
アイディアを出す present an idea
この新製品を売り込むための何かいいアイディアを出してくれませんか? Could you present some good ideas for promoting this new product?
アイディアを盗む steal an idea
アイディアがあふれ出る be full of ideas
アイディアがわく ideas rush/flood into a person's mind
彼の頭には次から次へと、斬新なアイディアがわいてくるようだ。It seems fresh ideas rush into his mind one after another.

足
foot, leg

足を引っぱる stand/get in a person's way
私たちは、互いの足を引っぱり合うことをやめて、解決法を考えるべきだ。We should stop finding fault

with one another and work out some solutions.

足が向く one's feet head on their own (to ...)

つい元ガールフレンドのアパートに、足が向いてしまった。Without realizing it, I started walking to my ex-girlfriend's apartment.

足を洗う wash one's hands (of ...); cut one's ties (with/to ...)

彼は、暴力団から足を洗う決心をした。He decided to cut his ties with the gang.

足を伸ばす go on (to someplace farther)

せっかく下関まで来たんだから、足を伸ばして博多まで行ってみよう。Since we've come all the way to Shimonoseki, let's go on to Hakata.

足を運ぶ go; visit

彼は私が入院していた病院に、何度か足を運んでくれた。He visited me several times in the hospital.

足を踏み入れる set foot (in ...); go into ...; enter

彼女は25歳のとき、政治の世界に足を踏み入れた。She went into politics at age 25.

足を組む cross one's legs

足がすくむ one's legs freeze (from fear)

足が棒になる one's legs become stiff (from walking, standing, etc.)

頭
brains, mind

頭を使う use one's brain/head

頭が下がる take off one's hat (to ...)

彼の謙虚な姿勢には、まったく頭が下がる。I really have to take my hat off to him for his humble manner.

頭を冷やす cool off

一晩頭を冷やしてから、決断を下すことにしよう。I should cool off overnight before making a decision.

頭に浮かぶ come to mind

時間切れ寸前に、いい考えが頭に浮かんだ。A good idea came to me just before I ran out of time.

頭に思い浮かべる think of ...; be reminded of ...; imagine

頭を下げる apologize (to ...)

頭をひねる rack one's brains

彼らは何か解決策はないかと、頭をひねった。They racked their brains to find some solutions.

頭を抱える tear one's hair out (over ...)

その支援団体のメンバーは、資金難に頭を抱えている。The members of the support group are tearing their hair out over lack of funds.

頭に入れておく keep something in mind

意味
meaning,
significance

意味がわかる／意味を理解する understand; know the meaning/significance (of ...)

私が言っていることの意味がわかりますか？ Do you understand what I'm saying?

意味を調べる look up the meaning (of ...)

この単語の意味を辞書で調べてごらん。Look up this word in your dictionary.

意味を取り違える misunderstand

意味を考える think over the meaning/significance (of ...)

私は彼が残したメッセージの意味を考えた。I thought over the meaning of the message he left for me.

意味を説明する explain the meaning (of ...)

イメージ
image,
impression

イメージをもつ have an impression (of ...)

私たちの多くは、その国についていいイメージをもっていない。Many of us don't have a positive impression of the country.

イメージが変わる one's image changes

茶髪にして、彼女はすっかりイメージが変わった。She looks completely different with her hair dyed brown.

イメージがわく can imagine

私には、その遠く離れた国がどんなところなのか、イメージがわかない。I can't imagine what that far-away country must be like.

イメージがよく［悪く］なる improve [harm] the image (of ...)

これらのテレビ CM で、我が社のイメージがよくなることを期待しています。We hope these TV commercials will improve our company's image.

うそ
lie

うそをつく tell a lie
私にそんな見え透いたうそをついても、無駄だよ。It's no use telling me such an obvious lie.

うそがばれる a lie is exposed
うそがばれて、彼は同僚の信用をなくした。He lost trust among his colleagues after his lie was exposed.

うそを見破る detect a lie

うそをつき通す keep telling a lie

疑い
doubt,
suspicion

疑いを抱く have doubts; feel/harbor doubt
彼女はその薬の効能に、疑いを抱き始めた。She began to have doubts about the effectiveness of the medicine.

疑いをかける suspect
あらぬ疑いをかけられて、本当に迷惑しています。I've been groundlessly suspected and it's really annoying.

疑いを晴らす clear up/resolve a doubt/doubts
彼女の証言が、私にかけられた疑いを晴らしてくれるだろう。Her testimony should clear me of suspicion.

疑いを招く arouse/raise suspicion
あなたがこれ以上言い訳しても、周囲の疑いを招くだけです。You can keep making excuses, but it will only raise suspicion among those around you.

疑いの余地がない be beyond a shadow of a doubt
彼に音楽の才能があるということには、疑いの余地がない。There's no doubt that he has musical talent.

腕
arm, ability,
skills

腕を組む fold one's arms
彼は腕を組んで、じっと考え事をしていた。He was lost in thought with his arms folded.

腕をまくる／腕まくりをする roll up one's sleeves

腕を上げる improve one's skill
彼は最近、めきめきゴルフの腕を上げている。His

golf skills have improved remarkably lately.

腕をふるう show one's ability; show off one's skills
かれ は日本で、ホテルの経営者として腕をふるっている。He is showing his ability as a hotel manager in Japan.

腕を磨く polish (up) one's skill
彼女は毎週、料理学校に通って、料理の腕を磨いた。She attended a cooking school every week to polish up her cooking skills.

腕によりをかける put all one's skills (into ...)
母は腕によりをかけて、クリスマスディナーを作った。My mother put all her cooking skills into making Christmas dinner.

腕が落ちる one's skills get rusty

腕をこまねく sit/stand there doing nothing; sit/stand there helplessly
彼らの横暴を、ただ腕をこまねいて見ているわけにはいきません。We just can't overlook their high-handed manners.

うわさ
rumor, gossip

うわさをする gossip; say things about ...
うわさをすれば影で、ほら、アキラがやって来た。Speak of the devil, here comes Akira.
クラスメートたちはみな、その新任の先生のうわさをしている。My classmates are saying things about the new teacher.

うわさを立てる start a rumor
そんな根も葉もないうわさを立てたのは誰なんだ？Who started such a groundless rumor?

うわさを広める spread/circulate a rumor

うわさに聞く hear about/of ...
その新しいフランス料理店のことは、うわさには聞いているが、まだ試したことはない。I've heard about the new French restaurant, but I've not tried it yet.

うわさになる there is a rumor (that ...); it is rumored that ...

二人の関係は、会社中のうわさになっている。The relationship between the two is the talk of the whole company.

うわさが飛び交う rumors fly (back and forth)

そのスキャンダルをめぐっては、いろいろなうわさが飛び交っている。There are a lot of rumors going around about the scandal.

うわさを否定する deny a rumor

うわさを流す spread/circulate a rumor

彼こそが学校中にそのうわさを流した張本人だ。He is the very person who spread the rumor throughout the school.

運
luck, fortune

運を試す try one's luck

運が尽きる run out of luck

我々の運も尽きたようだ。It seems we have run out of luck.

運に任せる leave things to chance

もうこうなったら、運に任せるしかない。All we can do now is leave the matter to fate.

運を占う tell a person's fortune

運が向いてくる one's luck turns/changes

彼らは十分な準備をして、運が向いてくるのをじっと待った。They prepared as well as they could, then waited for luck to turn in their favor.

顔
face

顔を売る make oneself known (to ...)

顔を出す／見せる turn up; show up

その晩のパーティーに、彼は1時間遅れて顔を出した。He turned up at the party one hour late that night.

顔を立てる save (a person's) face

ここはどうか私の顔を立てると思って、私の言うとおりにしてくれ。Please do as I tell you so I can save face.

顔をほころばせる break into a smile

孫娘を見るなり、彼は顔をほころばせた。He broke into a smile the moment he saw his granddaughter.

(…の)顔に泥を塗る bring shame on a person

両親の顔に泥を塗るようなことはできない。I can't do anything that will bring shame on my parents.

肩
shoulder

肩をすくめる shrug (one's shoulders)
　彼にその事実を指摘したけれど、彼は肩をすくめるだけだった。I pointed out the fact to him, but he just shrugged (his shoulders).

肩で風を切る swagger
　彼は社長になってから、会社の中を肩で風を切って歩き回っている。He has been swaggering about in our company since he became president.

肩を落とす drop one's shoulders in disappointment
　彼はテストの結果を見て、がっくりと肩を落とした。His shoulders dropped in disappointment when he saw the results of the exam.

肩をもつ take a person's side; take sides with ...
　父はいつも妹の肩をもってばかりいる。My father is always taking sides with my younger sister.

肩をいからせる square one's shoulders

気
mind

気をつける take care (of .../to do); mind; watch out
　気をつけて！ 階段が急だから。Be careful! The stairs are steep.

気にする mind; care (about ...); worry (about ...)
　兄は髪型のことは、あまり気にしない。My older brother doesn't care much about his hairstyle.
　済んでしまったことを気にしてもしかたがない。It's no use worrying about what is done.

気にかける care about ...; something is always on one's mind

気をきかせる take in the situation; play it smart
　彼女は気をきかせて、部屋を出て行ってくれた。She took in the situation and left the room, thankfully.

気を回す worry (about ...)
　彼女はあれこれ気を回しすぎて、とうとう神経が参ってしまった。She worried too much and finally broke down.

気を落とす be discouraged/disappointed

気を落とすなよ。何とかなるさ。Don't let it get you down. Things will work out somehow.

気を引く draw a person's attention

気を紛らす divert/distract oneself

彼はボウリングに行って、気を紛らした。He diverted himself by going bowling.

記憶
memory

記憶を呼び覚ます arouse/stir up one's memory

そのアニメは、私の子供時代の記憶を呼び覚ました。The anime film reminded me of my childhood.

記憶がよみがえる memory recurs (to a person/to a person's mind)

その古い写真を見て、事故の記憶がまざまざとよみがえった。Vivid memories of the accident recurred to my mind when I saw the old picture.

記憶がある remember; have a memory (of ...)

ずっと前に、この寺を訪れた記憶があります。I remember visiting this temple a long time ago.

記憶がない／記憶にない don't remember; don't have a memory (of ...)

彼には、事故前後に起きた出来事の記憶がないようだ。It seems that he has no memory of events that occurred before and after the accident.

記憶を新たにする refresh one's memory

記憶にとどめる keep ... in one's mind

記憶に残る be remembered; register (with a person); be memorable

マイケル・ジャクソンの名は、史上最も偉大なミュージシャンの一人として、人々の記憶に残るだろう。Michael Jackson will be remembered as one of the greatest musicians in history.

記憶に新しい be (still) fresh in one's mind

その選手の北京オリンピックでの活躍は、まだ私たちの記憶に新しい。The athlete's great achievements in the Beijing Olympics are still fresh in our minds.

記憶をたどる search one's memory

彼は記憶をたどりながら、その晩起きたことを私たちに話し始めた。He searched his memory and began to tell us what happened that night.

希望
hope, wishes

希望がある［ない］ have a wish [no wish]

配達日のご希望があれば、事前にご連絡ください。Please contact us beforehand if you have any requests concerning the delivery date.

希望を持つ have (a) hope

私たちは、彼が生存しているというかすかな希望をまだ持っています。We still have a faint hope that he is alive.

希望を抱く have hope; cherish a hope

マイクは、エミリーが自分と結婚してくれるという希望をまだ抱いている。Mike still cherishes a hope that Emily will marry him.

希望を捨てる give up/abandon (one's) hope

苦しい時にも、彼は決して希望を捨てなかった。He never gave up hope even in hard times.

希望を打ち砕く shatter a person's hope

その通知は、彼の希望を無惨に打ち砕いた。His hope was cruelly shattered by the notice.

希望を失う lose hope

希望にそう fulfill a person's wishes

最大限の努力をしますが、すべてのご希望にはそえないかもしれません。We'll give it our best efforts, but we may not be able to fulfill all of your wishes.

希望がかなう one's wish comes true; have one's wishes realized/fulfilled

希望がかなって、彼女はアメリカに留学する機会を得た。She got the chance to study in the United States as she had hoped.

希望に燃える be full of hope

彼は希望に燃えて、大学に進学した。He went on to college full of hope.

希望がわく hope rises

彼の演説を聞きながら、私は心の中に希望がわいてくるのを感じた。I felt hope swelling in my heart as I listened to his speech.

希望に満ちている be full of hope

義務
duty, obligation

義務がある be under (an) obligation

すべての市民には、納税の義務がある。All the citizens are under an obligation to pay taxes.

義務がない be under no obligation

私たちには、その会議に出席する義務はない。We're under no obligation to attend the meeting.

義務を果たす do one's duty

あなたがたは親としての義務を果たすよう、いっそうの努力をすべきです。You should make greater efforts to do your duty as parents.

義務を逃れる shirk/get out of one's duty

彼はあの手この手を尽くして、自分の義務を逃れようとした。He did whatever he could to shirk his duties.

義務を怠る neglect one's duty

義務を負わせる impose a duty (on a person); obligate someone

気持ち
feeling

気持ちがわかる／（人の）気持ちを理解する know how a person feels

君の気持ちはわかるが、彼の言い分も聞こうじゃないか。I know how you feel, but let's hear what he has to say.

（人の）気持ちを傷つける hurt a person's feelings

彼の不用意な発言が、彼女の気持ちを傷つけてしまった。His careless remark hurt her feelings.

（人の）気持ちになる (try to) know how a person feels

気持ちを込める put (all) one's heart (into ...)

気持ちを伝える convey one's feelings (to ...)

私は彼女に、ただ自分の気持ちを伝えたかっただけなのです。I just wanted to convey my feelings to her.

気持ちを打ち明ける open one's heart; open up

気持ちを整理する try to accept things; try to come to terms with the situation

口
mouth

口にする mention
彼はあまり自分の故郷のことを口にしたがらない。
He is reluctant to talk about his hometown.

口をはさむ interrupt; cut in
彼女は私たちの会話に、よく口をはさむ。She often cuts in on our conversations.

口をきく speak; talk; use one's influence
先生に向かってそんな口をきいてはいけないよ。
You shouldn't talk like that to your teacher.

口に出す express

口を出す meddle (in ...); stick one's nose (into ...)
彼は何にでも口を出すから、嫌いだ。I don't like him because he sticks his nose into everything.

口がすべる let ... slip
すみません、つい口がすべったのです。I'm sorry. It was just a slip of the tongue.

口が過ぎる say too much; go too far in what one says
ごめんよ。ちょっと口が過ぎたみたいだ。I'm sorry. It looks like I went too far in what I said.

口をそろえる say in chorus/unison
彼の友人たちはみな口をそろえて、「彼はそんなことをする人ではない」と言った。His friends said in chorus, "He would never do such a thing."

口をつぐむ clam up
事件の真相について、彼は口をつぐんだままだ。He is keeping his mouth shut about (the truth of) the incident.

口を割る confess; come out with ...
容疑者は当分口を割りそうにない。The suspect is not likely to confess for a while.

口をすぼめる pucker (up) one's lips
口をとがらす pout one's lips

首
neck

首が回らない be up to one's ears/neck (in ...)
彼は借金で首が回らないという話だよ。I hear he is in debt up to his ears.

首を縦に振る nod one's head; say yes
彼は私たちの訴えに、首を縦に振ろうとしなかった。He would not say yes to our request.

首を突っ込む stick one's nose (in ...)
人の話に首を突っ込まないでよ。Don't stick your nose into other people's business.

首を長くする wait eagerly/impatiently
彼女は来月のオーストラリア旅行を、首を長くして待っている。She can't wait for her trip to Australia next month.

首を横に振る shake one's head; refuse
私が一緒に行こうと申し出たが、彼は首を横に振った。I offered to go along with him, but he shook his head.

首をかしげる wonder
彼女はどうやってその情報を手に入れたのだろう、と彼は首をかしげた。He wondered how she got the information.

首をひねる think hard
彼の発言の意図は何だろう、と私たちはみな首をひねった。We all thought hard over what he meant by that statement.

行動
action, behavior

行動をとる take action
上司の命令を無視して、勝手な行動をとるわけにはいきません。I can't ignore an order from my boss and go my own way.

行動を起こす take action
CO₂削減のために、私たちはできるだけ早く行動を起こさなければなりません。We must take action as soon as possible to reduce CO_2 emissions.

行動に移す put ... into action; take action

声
voice, opinion

声を上げる express one's opinion; raise a cry (of ...); wail; raise one's voice

私たちは社会の偏見を正すために、反対の声を上げるべきだ。We should raise a cry of protest to eliminate prejudices in our society.

母親の顔を見ると、その少年は声を上げて泣き始めた。The boy began to wail when he saw his mother.

声をひそめる lower one's voice

上司がオフィスに入ってくると、社員は声をひそめた。The employees lowered their voices when their boss came into the office.

声をかける call out (to a person)

困ったことがあったら、いつでも私に声をかけてください。Please let me know anytime you have trouble.

声を荒げる raise one's voice

彼は声を荒げて、部下の一人をしかりつけた。He yelled at one of his staff in an angry voice.

声を詰まらせる choke

何度も悲しみに声を詰まらせながら、彼女は弔辞を述べた。She gave a eulogy in a voice often choked with grief.

声が震える／声を震わせる one's voice shakes

法廷で証言をしたとき、彼はずっと怒りで声が震えていた。His voice was shaking with anger as he gave testimony in the court.

声を大にする emphasize

若いときにたくさんの本を読むべきだと、声を大にして言いたい。I strongly advise that you read a lot of books when you are young.

言葉
words

言葉にする express; describe; put ... into words

今の気持ちを言葉にすることができません。I can't express how I feel now.

言葉を選ぶ choose one's words

彼は慎重に言葉を選びながら、その質問に答えた。He answered the question, choosing his words carefully.

言葉を交わす exchange words (with ...)

　私たちは会議の前に二三、言葉を交わした。We exchanged a few words before the meeting.

言葉を失う be (left) speechless/dumbfounded

　私は、彼が突然亡くなったと聞いて、言葉を失った。

The news of his sudden death left me speechless.

言葉が通じる be understood

　スペインを旅行中、彼は地元の人々となかなか言葉が通じなかった。While traveling in Spain, he had great difficulty in communicating with the local people.

言葉にできない beyond description/expression/words; be indescribable

　夕日に映える山々は、言葉にできないほど美しかった。The mountains glowing in the evening sun were beautiful beyond description.

言葉に詰まる be at a loss for words

　デートに遅れた理由をガールフレンドに聞かれて、彼は言葉に詰まった。He was at a loss for words when his girlfriend asked him why he was late for their date.

言葉を濁す speak vaguely

　記者からの質問に、彼は言葉を濁した。He gave a vague answer to the reporter's question.

舌
tongue

舌を巻く be astonished

　私たちは彼の独創的なアイディアに舌を巻いた。

We were astonished at his original idea.

舌を出す stick/put one's tongue out

舌が回る be eloquent/talkative

　いざスピーチする時になって、彼は突然舌が回らなくなった。When it was his turn to make a speech, he suddenly got tongue-tied.

失敗
failure, mistake

失敗する make a mistake; fail

　彼は事業に失敗して、一文無しになった。His business failed and he went broke.

失敗に終わる end in failure

我々の会社を乗っ取ろうとする彼らの企みは、失敗に終わった。Their plot to take over our company ended in failure.

失敗を繰り返す repeat a failure/mistake

失敗を恐れる be afraid of failure/making a mistake

失敗を恐れていては、何事も成功しない。You won't succeed in anything as long as you're afraid of failure.

尻
bottom,
buttocks

尻をたたく press; urge; encourage

両親に尻をたたかれて、彼はようやく受験勉強に身を入れ始めた。Urged by his parents, he finally put his heart into preparing for the entrance examination.

尻に火がつく be pressed for time; be forced to do something that one has been avoiding/putting off

彼は尻に火がつくまで、仕事に手を付けようとしない。He never settles down to work until the last minute.

尻ぬぐいをする make up for ...; clean/pick up (after) someone's mess

弟が事業に失敗したあと、結局私が尻ぬぐいをする羽目になった。After my brother's business failed, I had to clean up after his mess.

尻を振る wiggle one's hips

真実
truth

真実を語る tell the truth

彼は近いうちに真実を語ると、私たちに約束した。He promised us he would tell the truth soon.

真実を曲げる distort the truth

日本のメディアが真実を曲げて報道している理由をあなたは知っていますか？ Do you know the reason why the Japanese media is distorting the truth?

真実を突き止める find out the truth; get at the truth

事件の真実を突き止めてこそ、私たちは使命を果たしたことになる。We will only accomplish our mission by finding out the truth in this case.

真実を知る learn the truth

信頼 (しんらい)
trust,
confidence

信頼(しんらい)する trust; have trust/confidence (in ...)

彼(かれ)は責任感(せきにんかん)が強(つよ)いから、信頼(しんらい)してよい。You can trust him. He has a strong sense of responsibility.

信頼(しんらい)を得(え)る win a person's trust/confidence

その投手(とうしゅ)は試合(しあい)に完投(かんとう)して、監督(かんとく)の信頼(しんらい)を得(え)た。The pitcher won the manager's confidence by pitching a complete game.

信頼(しんらい)を失(うしな)う lose a person's trust/confidence

信頼(しんらい)を取(と)り戻(もど)す restore/regain a person's trust/confidence

その食品(しょくひん)メーカーは、消費者(しょうひしゃ)の信頼(しんらい)を取(と)り戻(もど)すのに必死(ひっし)だ。The food manufacturer is trying hard to restore confidence in consumers.

信頼(しんらい)を裏切(うらぎ)る betray a person's trust

信頼(しんらい)を置(お)く have confidence (in ...)

部長(ぶちょう)は部下(ぶか)たちに全幅(ぜんぷく)の信頼(しんらい)を置(お)いている。The manager has full confidence in his staff.

信頼(しんらい)にこたえる live up to a person's trust

大統領(だいとうりょう)は、国民(こくみん)の信頼(しんらい)にこたえるために全力(ぜんりょく)を尽(つ)くした。The president did his best to live up to the people's trust.

信頼関係(しんらいかんけい)を築(きず)く establish a bond of trust

背 (せ)
back

背(せ)を向(む)ける turn one's back (on ...)

その国(くに)は国際社会(こくさいしゃかい)の訴(うった)えに背(せ)を向(む)けた。The country turned its back on appeals from the international community.

背(せ)にする with one's back to ...

私(わたし)は記念碑(きねんひ)を背(せ)にして、写真(しゃしん)を1枚(いちまい)撮(と)ってもらった。I had my photo taken with the monument in the background.

背(せ)を丸(まる)める hunch one's back; hunch over

冷(つめ)たい北風(きたかぜ)が吹(ふ)く中(なか)を、私(わたし)たちはみな背(せ)を丸(まる)めて歩(ある)き続(つづ)けた。We all walked on with our backs hunched in the harsh north wind.

責任
responsibility

責任がある have (a) responsibility

私たちには、伝統文化を守り伝えていく責任がある。
We have a responsibility to preserve and pass on our traditional culture.

責任がない have no responsibility; be not responsible

その事故について、私には一切責任がない。I have no responsibility for the accident.

責任をとる take responsibility (for ...)

彼は不祥事の責任をとって、市長を辞職した。He took responsibility for the scandal and resigned as mayor.

責任を果たす fulfill one's responsibility

君は最後まで責任を果たすべきだ。You should fulfill your responsibilities to the end.

責任を逃れる avoid/evade responsibility

責任を逃れようとするなんて、彼らしくない。It is not like him to try to avoid responsibility.

責任を感じる feel responsible (for ...)

今回の騒ぎには、責任を感じています。I feel responsible for this confusion.

責任を問われる be held to blame (for ...); be held responsible (for ...)

飲酒運転による事故では、車の同乗者も責任を問われることがある。Fellow passengers can be held to blame for accidents caused by drunk driving.

責任をなすりつける put one's responsibility onto/on someone else

世話
care

世話をする look after ...; take care of ...

二人の息子が交代で、年老いた両親の世話をしている。The two sons take turns taking care of their old parents.

世話になる be helped; stay (with .../at ...)

この度は大変お世話になりました。Thank you so much for everything.

リサは夏休み中、パリのおばさんの家に世話になっ

た。Lisa stayed with her aunt in Paris during summer vacation.

世話を焼く look after ...; take care of ...; meddle in ...
　人の世話を焼く前に、自分のやるべきことをやりなさい。Mind your own business and don't meddle in other people's affairs.

世話を任せる leave ... in a person's charge/care

世話を頼む ask someone to take care of something/someone

想像
imagination

想像する imagine
　その宮殿は、想像していたよりずっと大きかった。The palace was much bigger than I had imagined.

想像を絶する be beyond all imagination
　その城の壮麗さは、想像を絶するものだった。The splendor of the castle was beyond all imagination.

想像をたくましくする give free rein/play to one's imagination
　少年は想像をたくましくして、宇宙船の絵を描いた。The boy drew a picture of a spaceship, giving free rein to his imagination.

想像に任せる leave ... to a person's imagination

想像がつく can guess/imagine
　彼らが何を企んでいるか、私には想像がつく。I can guess what they are planning to do.

想像力
imagination

想像力を働かせる use one's imagination
　想像力を働かせることによって、毎日の生活をもっとおもしろいものにすることができる。By using our imagination, we can make daily life more interesting.

想像力をかきたてる stimulate one's imagination
　その洞窟の壁画は、彼の想像力をかきたてた。The paintings in the cave stimulated his imagination.

想像力を駆使する give free rein/play to one's imagination

相談
consultation

相談する consult; talk to ...
　住民登録の手続きのことで、市役所に相談するつ

もりです。I'm going to consult the municipal office about the resident registration procedure.

ちょっと相談したいことがあるのですが。I have something I want to talk to you about.

相談を受ける be consulted/talked to

友人からペットのしつけのことで、よく相談を受ける。I'm often consulted by my friends about how to train pets.

相談を持ちかける consult

彼女は知り合いの弁護士に、その件について相談を持ちかけた。She consulted a lawyer friend about the matter.

相談に乗る give a person advice; lend someone an ear

彼ならいつでも喜んで相談に乗ってくれるでしょう。He will gladly give you advice anytime.

相談に応じる give a person advice

力
ちから
power, energy, ability

力を入れる put effort (into ...); put emphasis (on ...)

我が校では、実践的な英語教育に力を入れています。Our school puts emphasis on practical English education.

力を抜く relax

先生は私に肩の力を抜くように言った。The teacher told me to relax my shoulders.

力を込める strain; put strength (into ...)

力がつく gain strength; one's ability (in ...) improves

1年間で彼女はずいぶん日本語を書く力がついた。Her Japanese writing ability improved greatly in one year.

力をつける build up one's strength

力を発揮する show one's ability

彼はそのプロジェクトで、私たちが期待していた以上の力を発揮した。He showed more ability in the project than we had expected.

力を合わせる work together; cooperate; make a united effort (to do)

我々は、力を合わせて、この難局を乗り切らなければなりません。We must work together to get through this crisis.

力を使い果たす spend/use up all one's energy

そのマラソン選手は、レース前半で力を使い果たしてしまったようだ。It seems the marathon runner used up all his energy in the first half of the race.

力を注ぐ focus one's efforts (on ...)

その大国は国内の天然資源開発に力を注いでいる。The big country is focusing its efforts on developing domestic natural resources.

力を蓄える save one's energy

来週の試合に向けて、力を蓄えておくべきだ。We should save our energies for the game next week.

力が尽きる have all one's energy used up; run out of energy

力がわく be filled with energy/strength

しっかり朝食を食べたら力がわいてきた。The nutritious breakfast filled me with energy.

力を借りる seek a person's help

私たちはその問題の解決に、技術専門家の力を借りることにした。We decided to ask the help of technical experts to solve the problem.

力を貸す help someone; give someone help

力になる help

困ったときは、遠慮なく私に電話してください。いつでも力になりますよ。Don't hesitate to call me when you're in trouble. I'll be ready to help anytime.

力が及ぶ be within one's ability/power

力が及ぶ限り、あなたを支援します。We'll assist you as best we can.

司法試験に何度か挑戦したが、力が及ばなかった。I've tried to pass the bar examination several times, but it was too much for me.

知識(ちしき) knowledge	知識を広(ひろ)げる expand one's knowledge 知識を得(え)る acquire/get knowledge 　百科事典(ひゃっかじてん)は、幅広(はばひろ)い知識(ちしき)を得(え)るのに役立(やくだ)つでしょう。Encyclopedias can help you acquire a wide range of knowledge. 知識を吸収(きゅうしゅう)する absorb knowledge 　子供(こども)は知識(ちしき)を吸収(きゅうしゅう)するのが非常(ひじょう)に速(はや)い。Children absorb knowledge very quickly. 知識を身(み)につける acquire/get knowledge 知識を増(ふ)やす increase/improve one's knowledge 　できるだけ多(おお)くの本(ほん)を読(よ)んで、知識(ちしき)を増(ふ)やすことが大切(たいせつ)です。It is important to increase your knowledge by reading as many books as you can.
チャンス chance, opportunity	チャンスをつかむ seize a chance/an opportunity 　その俳優(はいゆう)は再起(さいき)のチャンスをつかんだ。The actor seized an opportunity to make a comeback. チャンスを逃(のが)す miss a chance/an opportunity 　彼(かれ)は大手(おおて)自動車(じどうしゃ)メーカーに就職(しゅうしょく)する絶好(ぜっこう)のチャンスを逃(のが)した。He missed a golden opportunity to get a job with a major automaker. チャンスが巡(めぐ)ってくる get a/the chance 　ようやく彼(かれ)に外国留学(がいこくりゅうがく)のチャンスが巡(めぐ)ってきた。He finally got a chance to study abroad. チャンスをものにする take advantage of an opportunity 　ビジネスの成功(せいこう)は、巡(めぐ)ってきたチャンスをいかにものにするかで決(き)まる。Taking advantage of opportunities that present themselves is key to success in business.
注意(ちゅうい) attention	注意(ちゅうい)する pay attention (to ...); be careful 　通(とお)りを渡(わた)るときは、注意(ちゅうい)してね。Be careful when you cross the road. 注意を払(はら)う pay attention (to ...) 　あなたはパスワードの管理(かんり)に、もっと注意(ちゅうい)を払(はら)うべきだ。You should pay more attention to the man-

agement of your passwords.

注意が足りない be careless

ドアの鍵をかけ忘れるなんて、あなたは注意が足りませんよ。 It was careless of you not to lock the door.

注意が行き届く take very good care (of ...); take careful steps to ...

手
hand

手を貸す lend someone a hand

この机を動かしたいんだけど、手を貸してもらえる？

I want to move this desk. Could you lend me a hand?

手を借りる get someone's help

手に入れる get; obtain

手に入る get; be available

そのグループはとても人気があるので、コンサートのチケットがなかなか手に入らない。 Tickets for the group's concerts are hard to get because they are so popular.

手が込む be elaborate

手が出る cannot resist something

のどから手が出るほど、そのコンサートのチケットが欲しい。 I would die to get a ticket to the concert.

おなかいっぱいでも、甘い物にはついつい手が出てしまう。 I cannot resist sweets even when I'm full.

手が出ない cannot afford

家賃20万円のマンションなど、とても手が出ない。

I can't possibly afford an apartment with a rent of 200,000 yen a month.

手が届く be within one's reach; can afford

1万円のネックレスなら、私にも手が届く。 Even I can afford a 10,000-yen necklace.

手を打つ do something; make a move

これ以上は、手の打ちようがありません。 There's nothing more we can do now.

手を出す (actively) get involved in something; try to steal something; resort to force; seduce

俺の女に手を出すな。 Keep your hands off my girlfriend.

手に取る　pick up; take ... in one's hands
　こちらの指輪をお手に取って、よくごらんくださ
い。Please take these rings in your hand and have a
good look.

手を切る　break things off (with ...)

手を組む　join (with ...)

手をこまねく　do nothing
　彼女が本当に助けを必要としていたとき、彼はただ
手をこまねいて見ていた。When she really needed
help, he just sat back and did nothing.

手をつける　touch; start (doing) something
　彼は出された食事にまったく手をつけなかった。He
didn't even touch the meal set in front of him.

手を抜く　cut corners (in one's job, etc.)
　私は仕事では、決して手を抜きません。I never cut
corners in my job.

手を焼く　be too much for ...; have trouble doing something
　私たちはゴミを漁りに来るカラスに、手を焼いてい
ます。We just can't stop the crows from raiding the
garbage.

手を挙げる　raise one's hand

手を握る　hold a person's hand; shake hands

手をつなぐ　join hands
　二人の子供たちは、手をつないで歩いていた。The
two children were walking hand in hand.

手をかざす　put/hold one's hands over ...

手を振る　wave (one's hands)

度胸
courage, nerve

度胸がある［ない］have courage [no courage]; have
guts [no guts]
　私には、スカイダイビングに挑戦する度胸はない。I
don't have the courage to try skydiving.

度胸を決める　work up one's courage
　彼は度胸を決めて、彼女にプロポーズした。He worked

up his courage and proposed to her.

度胸がすわる have a lot of courage/guts; have nerves
of steel

彼女はまだ10歳だが、実に度胸がすわっている。

She is only 10, but she's really got a lot of courage.

度胸を試す test one's courage/nerve

ドジ
blunder

ドジをする make a blunder; screw up

ドジをやらかす make a blunder; screw up

彼は1日に1度は必ずドジをやらかす。He screws
up at least once every day.

ドジをしでかす make a blunder; screw up

ドジを踏む make a blunder; screw up

今度はドジを踏むなよ。Don't blow it this time!

馬鹿
fool,
foolishness

馬鹿にする make fun of someone; make a fool of someone

コンピューターが使えないからといって、誰も馬鹿
にしたりしない。Nobody will make fun of you just
because you can't use a computer.

馬鹿にならない cannot make light of something

1杯200円のコーヒーも、毎日飲むと馬鹿にならな
い。200 yen a day for coffee really adds up.

馬鹿(なこと)を言う talk nonsense

馬鹿を見る make a fool of oneself

彼の冗談を真に受けて、馬鹿を見た。I took his joke
seriously and made a fool of myself.

鼻
nose

鼻にかける be stuck up

彼女は金持ちだということを鼻にかけている。She
is stuck up about being rich.

鼻を突っ込む poke/stick one's nose into ...

他人の問題に鼻を突っ込むのは、やめたほうがいい。
You should stop sticking your nose into other people's affairs.

鼻をへし折る bring/take someone down a peg

鼻であしらう turn one's nose up at ...

昨日ナンパした女の子には、鼻であしらわれた。I

tried to pick up a girl yesterday, but she flatly turned
me down.

腹 stomach

腹を立てる get angry; lose one's temper

　彼が腹を立てたところを見たことがありません。

I've never seen him lose his temper.

腹を決める decide; make up one's mind

　彼は会社を辞めて、フリーでやっていくと腹を決め
た。He decided to leave the company and become a
freelancer.

腹をくくる be determined to do ...

腹を抱える double up with laughter

　彼はお笑いのDVDを見ながら、腹を抱えて笑って
いた。He doubled up with laughter watching the
comedy DVD.

腹を割る be frank (with a person)

　今日は腹を割って話そう。Let's talk frankly/openly
today.

(相手の)腹を探る find out a person's real intentions

秘密 secret

秘密を守る keep a secret

　彼はたぶん秘密を守れないだろうから、彼には言わ
ないでおくつもりだ。I'm not going to tell him because
he probably won't be able to keep it secret.

秘密をばらす disclose/reveal a secret

秘密を打ち明ける tell/confide one's secret to someone

　彼女は私にだけ秘密を打ち明けてくれた。She told
her secret just to me.

秘密を漏らす let secrets out (to someone); leak a secret

　いったい誰が秘密を漏らしたのだろう。I wonder who
leaked the secret.

秘密にする keep something (a) secret

　今話したことは、ここだけの秘密にしてください。

Please keep what I just said between you and me.

不満 dissatisfaction

不満を言う complain; grumble

不満を漏らす complain; grumble

　彼女は仕事の不満を漏らしたことがない。She has

People

never complained about her work.

不満をぶちまける vent one's frustration(s); air one's complaint(s)

かなり酔っ払っていた彼は、上司に仕事の不満をぶちまけた。 Being fairly drunk, he aired his complaints about his job to his boss.

不満がある［ない］have complaints [no complaints]

今度引っ越したアパートは快適で、何も不満はありません。 The apartment I recently moved into is very nice and I have no complaints.

雰囲気
atmosphere

雰囲気がいい［悪い］the atmosphere is good [bad]

この近くに、とても雰囲気がいいバーがあるんだ。これから行かない？ There's a bar with a good atmosphere near here. Why don't we go now?

雰囲気を壊す ruin the (good) atmosphere

コンビニやファーストフード店の派手な外観は、古い町並みの雰囲気を壊す。 The loud exteriors of convenience stores and fast-food restaurants ruin the good atmosphere of old houses and streets.

雰囲気になじむ get used to the atmosphere

雰囲気にのまれる be overwhelmed by the atmosphere

私はその場の雰囲気にのまれて、何も言うことができなかった。 I was overwhelmed by the atmosphere and couldn't say anything.

雰囲気を変える change the atmosphere

へま
blunder

へまをする／やる make a blunder/mistake

とんだへまをやってしまった。 I've made an awful blunder.

へまをやらかす make a blunder/mistake

彼はしょっちゅうへまをやらかして、上司に怒られている。 He often makes mistakes and gets reprimanded by his boss.

へまをしでかす make a blunder/mistake

偏見
prejudice

偏見がある there is prejudice/bias (against ...), have a prejudice/bias (against ...)

152

同性愛者に対して、この国ではまだ根深い偏見がある。There is still deep-rooted prejudice against homosexuals in this country.

偏見を持っている have a prejudice (against ...); be prejudiced/biased (against ...)

私は今時の女子高生に対して、偏見を持っていた。

I was biased against the high school girls of today.

偏見と闘う fight prejudice(s)

その団体は、エイズ患者に対する偏見と闘っています。That group is fighting prejudice against people with AIDS.

偏見をなくす eliminate/get rid of prejudice(s)

偏見にとらわれている be prejudiced/biased

偏見にとらわれていると、その映画を十分に楽しめないよ。If you go in with a biased view, of course you won't enjoy the movie.

偏見を抱く have a prejudice (against ...)

骨
bone

骨を折る take pains; go to trouble

鈴木さんは私のために、仕事を見つけたりアパートを探したりと、いろいろ骨を折ってくれました。Mr. Suzuki took pains to find me a job and an apartment.

骨が折れる be painstaking/difficult/hard

その大量のデータの移し替えは、なかなか骨が折れる仕事でした。Transferring all that data was pretty exhausting.

骨を埋める stay somewhere for the rest of one's life

彼は30年前、日本に骨を埋めるつもりでアメリカからやってきた。He came to Japan from the United States 30 years ago, hoping to make it his final home.

骨を休める take a (good) rest

今度の休みには温泉にでも行って、ゆっくり骨を休めてください。On your next holiday you should go to some hot-spring resort and take a good rest.

骨を惜しまない spare no effort

間違い
mistake, fault

間違いをする make a mistake
何度も同じ間違いをしないように、気をつけなさい。
Be careful not to repeat the same mistake.

間違いを犯す make a mistake

間違いをやらかす make a mistake

間違いを恐れる be afraid of making a mistake
間違いを恐れていては、外国語を話せるようにはならないよ。You'll never learn to speak a foreign language if you are afraid of making mistakes.

間違いを見つける discover a mistake
彼女はよく、私の作った書類の間違いを見つけてくれます。She often finds mistakes in the documents I create.

間違いを認める admit one's mistake/error
間違いを素直に認めてすぐに改めるのが、彼のいいところだ。The good thing about him is that he simply admits his mistakes and corrects them immediately.

間違いを隠す cover up one's mistake
友達の犯した間違いを隠そうとしたのが、彼の間違いだった。He was wrong to try to cover up his friend's mistake.

間違いを正す correct a mistake

間違いがある there is a mistake
私の記憶に間違いがなければ、彼はギリシャ出身です。If I remember correctly, he is from Greece.

間違いを繰り返す repeat a mistake

身
body

身が入る become absorbed in something; do something eagerly/seriously
試験が1週間後に迫っているのに、なぜか勉強に身が入らない。The exam is only a week away, but somehow I can't concentrate on studying.

身に覚えがある be conscious of doing something

身に付ける acquire; master
スイスで過ごした10年の間に、フランス語とイタリア語を身に付けました。I acquired French and Italian

during 10 years in Switzerland.

身を起こす rise

彼女は一介の主婦から身を起こして、ケータリングの会社の経営者になった。She rose from an ordinary housewife to run a catering company.

身を引く retire; resign; back out (of ...)

身を滅ぼす ruin oneself

その俳優は酒とドラッグで、身を滅ぼした。Alcohol and drugs led the actor to his ruin.

身を任せる give into ...; go with ...

彼はいつも流れに逆らわず、成り行きに身を任せているように見える。It seems that he never strives against the current and just goes with the flow.

身を寄せる stay with someone

彼女は離婚後しばらくの間は、実家に身を寄せていた。She stayed with her parents for a while after the divorce.

身を入れる put one's heart into ...; settle down to ...

身を立てる establish oneself (as ...)

身を持ち崩す something leads one to (one's) ruin

耳
ear

耳が痛い something/someone hits a sore spot; one's ears ache/hurt

それを言われると、耳が痛いよ。That hits a sore spot.

耳に入れる let someone know; tell

お耳に入れておきたいことがあるのですが。There's something I'd like to tell you.

耳に障る find something irritating/displeasing

耳にする hear

その名前は何度か耳にしたことがあります。I've heard that name several times.

耳にたこができる be fed up with hearing something; be tired of hearing something

その話は彼女から、耳にたこができるくらい聞かされた。She's told me the story so many times that I'm totally fed up with it.

耳に残る (still) ring in one's ears

耳を疑う cannot believe one's ears

　自分の名前が呼ばれたとき、私は自分の耳を疑った。

I couldn't believe my (own) ears when I heard my name called.

耳を貸す listen to someone

耳を貸さない turn a deaf ear (to ...)

　その会社との取引をやめるよう忠告したが、彼は耳を貸そうとしなかった。I told him to break off business with that company, but he turned a deaf ear to my advice.

耳を傾ける turn/give an attentive ear (to ...); listen intently (to ...)

耳を澄ます strain one's ears

　耳を澄ますと、遠くで笛や太鼓の音が聞こえた。When I strained my ears, I could hear the sounds of flutes and drums in the distance.

耳をそばだてる prick up one's ears

耳を塞ぐ plug/cover one's ears

胸
chest, heart

胸を張る keep one's chin up

胸が痛む feel sorry/sad

　その事故で家族を亡くした人々のことを考えると、胸が痛む。Thinking about those who have lost their families in the accident breaks my heart.

胸に秘める keep something to oneself

胸にしまう keep something to oneself

　このことは、私一人の胸にしまっておきます。I will keep this to myself and will tell it to nobody.

胸に刻む engrave something into one's mind/memory

胸を弾ませる one's heart leaps with (joy)

胸をふくらませる one's heart swells with (hope, etc.)

　子供たちはみんな、期待に胸をふくらませてその日を待った。All the children waited for the day, full of hope.

胸を焦がす burn with love (for ...)

胸をなで下ろす be relieved
彼のけががたいしたことはないとわかって、胸をなで下ろした。I was relieved to hear that his injury was not serious.

目
eye

目が覚める wake; be awakened
今朝は激しい風の音で目が覚めた。I woke up to the sound of intense wind this morning.

目を覚ます wake up
そろそろ目を覚まして、現実を直視すべきだ。It's about time you woke up and faced reality.

目が点になる one's eyes almost pop out; be agape
友人の結婚式に彼が着てきた服を見て、目が点になった。I was agape at the outfit he wore to our friend's wedding.

目が回る feel dizzy
1年のこの時期は、いつも目が回るほど忙しい。Usually, we are dizzyingly busy at this time of year.

目がくらむ be blinded/dazzled

目が据わる get a glazed look in one's eyes
私が店に着いたとき、彼はすでに酔っ払って目が据わっていた。When I got to the bar, he was already drunk and his eyes were glazing over.

目が離せない cannot take one's eyes off something
息子は歩き始めたばかりで、片時も目が離せません。My son just started to walk and I can't take my eyes off him even for a moment.

目からうろこが落ちる be (suddenly) awakened to the truth
酢が洗剤の代わりに使えると知って、目からうろこが落ちた。It was an eye-opener to learn that vinegar could be used as a detergent.

目に浮かぶ can clearly picture something

目にする see
私はそのキャンプ場で、信じられない光景を目にしました。I saw an incredible sight at the campground.

目につく (can) be seen easily

最近、その商品の広告がよく目につく。Recently, advertisements for that product can be seen everywhere.

目に入る see

目に留まる something catches one's eye

たまたまその本のタイトルが目に留まったので、買ってみた。The title of the book just caught my eye, so I bought it.

目を疑う cannot believe one's eyes

アパートに帰って電気をつけた瞬間、私は目を疑った。I got back to my apartment, turned on the light, and couldn't believe my eyes.

目を凝らす strain one's eyes; stare

目を盗む do something behind someone's back; do something when someone isn't looking

うちの猫は時々私の目を盗んで、アパートの部屋から脱走する。My cat sometimes escapes from the apartment when I'm not looking.

目を奪われる be fascinated

祭りの最大の見せ場である巨大な山車に、目を奪われた。I was fascinated by the huge floats, which are the main attraction of the festival.

目を配る watch carefully/closely

目を光らせる keep an eye out (for ...); keep a close eye on ...

近所の人たちは、私がゴミをきちんと分別しているか、目を光らせている。My neighbors keep a close eye on me to make sure I sort the garbage properly.

目を伏せる look down

目を離す turn one's eyes away

ちょっと目を離したすきに、ステーキを焦がしてしまった。The steak got burned when I turned my eyes away for a moment.

目を通す look/glance over ...; skim through ...

朝はあまり時間がないので、新聞はざっと目を通

す程度です。I just glance over the newspaper in the morning since I don't have much time.

面倒 trouble

面倒を見る take care of ...; look after ...

旅行で留守の間、友達の一人に飼い猫の面倒を見てもらった。I had a friend of mine take care of my cat while I was away on a trip.

面倒をかける cause someone trouble; trouble/bother someone

いつも面倒をかけてばかりで、本当にごめんなさい。I'm really sorry I've been causing you so much trouble.

面倒を起こす cause/make trouble

約束 promise, appointment

約束(を)する promise

危険なことはしないと約束してね。Promise me you won't do anything dangerous.

約束を守る keep one's promise

どんなことがあっても、約束は守ります。No matter what happens, I will keep my promise.

約束を破る break one's promise

彼が来ないのはおかしい。彼は約束を破るような人じゃないんだ。It's weird he hasn't come. He's not the kind of person who breaks a promise.

約束がある have an appointment

すみません、明日の夜は約束があってあなたのパーティーには行けません。Sorry, but I have an appointment tomorrow evening and can't come to your party.

約束を果たす fulfill one's promise

勇気 courage

勇気を出す pluck up one's courage

きっとうまくいくからやってみなよ。勇気を出して！Come on, you'll make it. Have guts!/Show some guts!/Be brave!

勇気を奮い起こす muster up all one's courage

勇気を振り絞る gather all one's courage

その女の子は、勇気を振り絞って男の子に告白した。The girl plucked up all her courage and told the boy that she liked him.

勇気をなくす lose one's courage; be discouraged

勇気を与える give someone courage

　彼女の挑戦は、多くの人に勇気を与えたと思います。

I think her attempt gave a lot of people courage.

勇気がわく be encouraged

　あなたの話を聞いていると、だんだん勇気がわいて

きた。Your story has given me a lot of courage.

勇気がある have courage (to do something)

　社長に直談判するとは、勇気があるね。It's very

courageous of you to negotiate directly with the pres-

ident.

夢
dream

夢を見る dream; have a dream

　私はよく空を飛んでいる夢を見ます。I often have a

dream in which I'm flying.

夢から覚める wake up from a dream

夢に出てくる appear/be in one's dream

　昨日ブラッド・ピットが夢に出てきた。Brad Pitt ap-

peared in my dream last night.

夢にも思わない not even dream of ...

　自分が三つ子の母親になるなんて、夢にも思わなかっ

た。I never dreamed I would become the mother of

triplets.

夢を持つ have a dream

夢を描く dream

　小さいころは、どんな夢を描いていましたか? What

sorts of dreams did you have when you were small?

夢を追い続ける keep pursuing/chasing one's dream

夢を叶える realize one's dream

　彼女はついに宇宙飛行士になるという夢を叶えた。

She realized her dream of becoming an astronaut at

last.

夢が叶う one's dream comes true

夢を実現させる realize one's dream

夢をあきらめる give up one's dream

夢を壊す destroy/ruin someone's dream

子供の夢を壊すようなことを言わないで。Don't say things that can ruin children's dreams.

夢を分析する analyze a dream

理解
understanding

理解を深める gain a deeper/better understanding (of something)

1週間のサマーキャンプで、学生たちは互いに理解を深めることができるでしょう。A week of summer camp will help promote mutual understanding among the students.

理解を示す show understanding (of something); show sympathy

彼らはこちら側の要求に対し、一定の理解を示した。They showed some sympathy toward our demands.

理解を得る gain understanding (from someone)

理解に苦しむ can hardly understand; something is hard to understand

彼女がなぜそんなことをしたのか、理解に苦しむ。I can't understand why she did such a thing.

SCHOOL & WORK

Entrance, Attendance & Graduation

学校 (がっこう)
school

学校に行く (がっこうにいく) go to school
学校を選ぶ (がっこうをえらぶ) choose a school
学校に入る／入学する (がっこうにはいる／にゅうがくする) enter a school
学校を出る (がっこうをでる) graduate from school
学校を出てから、いろいろな仕事を経験しました。(がっこうをでてから、いろいろなしごとをけいけんしました。)

I have experienced various jobs since I graduated from school.

学校をやめる (がっこうをやめる) quit school
彼は家庭の事情で、学校をやめなければならなかった。(かれはかていのじじょうで、がっこうをやめなければならなかった。) He had to quit school for family reasons.

学校を退学させられる (がっこうをたいがくさせられる) be expelled from school
学校を休む (がっこうをやすむ) be absent from school
学校を休学する (がっこうをきゅうがくする) be absent from school (for a certain period of time)
1年間学校を休学していたので、私はみんなより1つ年上だ。(いちねんかんがっこうをきゅうがくしていたので、わたしはみんなよりひとつとしうえだ。) I'm one year older than my classmates because I was absent from school for a year.

学校を変わる／移る／転校する (がっこうをかわる／うつる／てんこうする) change schools; go to another school

高校 (こうこう)
high school

高校に入る／入学する (こうこうにはいる／にゅうがくする) enter high school
高校を卒業する (こうこうをそつぎょうする) graduate from high school
高校をやめる／中退する (こうこうをやめる／ちゅうたいする) drop out of high school
高校を中退しても、大学を受験することはできる。(こうこうをちゅうたいしても、だいがくをじゅけんすることはできる。)

Even if you drop out of high school, you still have a chance to take a university entrance exam.

高校を休学する (こうこうをきゅうがくする) be absent from high school (for a certain period of time)

高校(の入試)に合格する pass the high school entrance exam

高校に合格したお祝いにiPhoneを買ってもらった。 I got an iPhone as a present to celebrate my passing the high school entrance exam.

高校(の)入試を受ける take a high school entrance exam

高校に(入学)願書を出す submit an application to a high school

授業料
school fees

授業料を払う pay school fees

授業料を納める pay school fees

4月末日までに、前期分の授業料を納めなければならない。 I need to pay the school fee for the first term by the end of April.

授業料を滞納する fall into arrears in paying school fees

授業料を滞納している生徒が、各クラスに数名ずついる。 There are a few students in each class who have fallen into arrears in paying school fees.

授業料の免除を申し込む request to be exempted from paying school fees

大学
college,
university

大学に進学する go on to college/university

私は経済学を勉強するために大学に進学しました。 I went on to college to study economics.

大学入試を受ける take a college entrance exam

大学に合格する pass a college entrance exam

大学に入学する enter college

大学を中退する／やめる drop out of college; quit college

兄はいったん大学を中退したが、弁護士を目指して25歳で別の大学に入り直した。 My brother once dropped out of college, but at age 25 he reentered another one in order to become a lawyer.

大学を卒業する graduate from college

去年京都の大学を卒業して、今年の6月から東京

で仕事をしています。I graduated from a college in Kyoto last year and have been working in Tokyo since this June.

単位
credit

大学を出る graduate from college

単位を取る earn credits; pass

単位を落とす fail to earn credits; fail

彼はロシア語の単位を落として、留年した。He failed to earn credits in Russian and was held back.

単位が足りない be short of credits

Classes & Classrooms

学生・生徒
student

生徒を当てる call on a student

その先生は、手を挙げていない生徒にも当てた。The teacher even called on students who were not raising a hand.

生徒を指す call on a student

生徒に問題を出す ask students a question

生徒に宿題を出す give students homework/an assignment

生徒をしかる scold a student

生徒に注意する warn a student

二日続けて遅刻した生徒に注意をした。I warned a student who came late for two days in a row.

生徒をほめる praise a student

生徒を指導する instruct/guide a student

生徒が遅刻する a student comes late to class

学級
class

学級委員を選ぶ choose a class representative

年度の初めに、学級委員を選ぶ選挙が行われます。A vote is held at the beginning of the school year to choose a class representative.

学級委員になる become a class representative

学級閉鎖になる class is suspended

今年の冬は、新型インフルエンザの影響で、学級閉

鎖になるクラスが続出した。Classes were suspended one after another due to the pandemic flu this winter.

教科書
textbook

教科書を開く open one's textbook

教科書の ７ ５ページを開いてください。Open your textbooks to page 75.

教科書を読む read one's textbook

教科書を忘れる forget to bring one's textbook

教科書を借りる borrow a textbook

隣のクラスの友達に数学の教科書を借りた。I borrowed the math textbook from a friend in the next class.

教科書に落書きをする scribble in a textbook

教室
classroom

教室に行く go to class

教室に入る enter/go into the classroom

教室を出る leave the classroom

教室を間違える go into the wrong classroom

大急ぎで飛び込んだら、教室を間違えていた。I rushed inside, only to find it was the wrong classroom.

教室に残る stay/remain in the classroom

教室を移動する move from one classroom to another

アメリカの学校では、毎時間生徒が教室を移動する。Students move from one room to another every class in schools in the United States.

教室の掃除をする clean the classroom

日本の学校ではふつう、生徒自身が教室の掃除をする。In Japanese schools, students themselves usually clean their classrooms.

クラス
class

クラスの人気者だ be popular in class

クラスがまとまっている the class is cohesive

合唱コンテストの練習をするうちに、だんだんクラスがまとまってきた。The class gradually came together as it practiced for the choir contest.

クラスをまとめる bring the class together

クラス（全員）で相談する discuss in the class

文化祭の出し物を何にするか、クラス全員で相談し

た。The whole class discussed what to feature in the school festival.

**黒板
blackboard**

黒板に書く／板書する write on the blackboard

日本語がまだあまりできないころは、先生が黒板に書いたものを写すだけでも大変だった。In the days when my Japanese was not so good, it was hard just to copy what the teacher wrote on the blackboard.

黒板を消す erase the blackboard

黒板(の説明)を写す copy what is written on the blackboard

黒板を拭く wipe/clean the blackboard

**試験・テスト
exam**

試験を受ける take an exam

試験に受かる pass an exam

試験に通る pass an exam

2度目の挑戦で、交換留学プログラムの試験に通った。I passed the exam for an exchange program on my second try.

試験に落ちる fail an exam

試験に出る be in an exam

ここはきっと試験に出るから、ポイントを押さえておきなさい。I'm pretty sure that this will be on the exam, so you should grasp what it means.

試験を採点する grade exam papers

**質問
question**

質問(を)する ask a question

昼休みに生徒が職員室まで質問しにきた。A student came to the teachers' room to ask questions during the lunch break.

質問に答える answer a question

質問を浴びせる fire questions one after another

質問攻めにあう be bombarded with questions

赴任した学校では、初日に生徒たちから質問攻めにあった。On the very first day at school, I was bombarded with questions from students.

質問を受け付ける answer questions

質問を受け流す evade/dodge questions

プライベートに関する質問は、軽く受け流した。I didn't take the questions related to my private affairs seriously.

授業
class

授業を受ける take a class

私は山田先生の授業は、一度も受けたことがありません。I have never taken a class with Mr. Yamada.

授業をする teach a class

授業をとる take a class; register for a class

授業をサボる cut/skip a class

高校時代には、たまに授業をサボって映画を見に行ったりした。During my high school days, I sometimes cut classes and went to see a movie.

授業に出る／出席する attend classes; be present in class

授業についていく keep up with the class

授業についていけない生徒のために、補習が行われている。Remedial lessons are offered for students who have difficulty in keeping up with the class.

授業中だ be in class

授業を休む／欠席する be absent from class

その先生は、1学期中に5回授業を休んだだけで、落第にするらしい。Apparently that teacher fails students who are absent from class only five times in a term.

授業に遅れる be late for class

授業の準備をする prepare for class

授業の予習をする prepare for class

授業の復習をする review for class

宿題
homework,
assignment

宿題が出る be given homework/assignments

こんなにたくさん宿題が出ると、せっかくの休みも楽しめない。We can't really enjoy the holidays with so much homework.

宿題をする do one's homework

宿題を済ませる finish one's homework

さっさと宿題を済ませて、遊びに行こうよ。Hurry

up and finish your homework. Let's go out and have fun.

宿題を提出する submit one's homework

宿題を忘れる forget to do one's homework

宿題がたまっている have a stack of unfinished homework

休みの間ほとんど遊んでいたので、宿題がどっさりたまっている。Since I idled away most of the vacation, I have a stack of unfinished homework.

成績
grades

成績が上がる one's grade improves

２学期になって英語の成績が上がった。My grade in English improved in the second term.

成績が下がる one's grade drops

成績が落ちる one's grade drops

成績が伸びる improve one's grade

成績が伸び悩む make little improvement in one's grade

成績が伸び悩んでいる生徒に、何かアドバイスをしてください。Give some advice to the students who are making little improvement in their grades.

いい［悪い］成績をとる get a good [bad] grade

席
seat, place

席につく take one's seat; be seated

さあ、みんな、席について。Now everybody, take your seat.

席を代わる change seats/places

目が悪いので、彼に席を代わってくれるよう頼んだ。I asked him to change seats with me because I have poor eyesight.

席を立つ leave one's seat

席替えをする change the seating arrangement/order

席替えをしたら、たまたま一番前の真ん中の席になった。The seating arrangement was changed and my seat ended up in the center of the front row.

席を取る keep/save one's seat/place

席に座る take a seat; sit down

先生・講師・教授 **teacher, professor**	先生に質問する ask the teacher questions 先生に相談する consult with one's teacher 　困ったことがあったら、先生に相談しなさい。If you 　have any trouble, talk to your teacher. 先生に聞く ask one's teacher 先生に教わる learn from one's teacher 　先生には数学だけでなく、いろいろなことを教わり 　ました。I learned from you not only math but many 　other things. 先生に習う learn from one's teacher 先生に推薦状を書いてもらう have one's teacher write 　one a letter of recommendation
ノート **note, notebook**	ノートをとる take/make notes 　みんな真剣にその講義のノートをとっていた。Every- 　one was seriously taking notes at the lecture. ノートを借りる borrow someone's notebook ノートを貸す lend one's notebook to someone 　昨日授業を休んでしまったので、ノートを貸しても 　らえますか？ Could I borrow your notebook since I 　was absent from class yesterday? ノートを写す copy someone's notebook
勉強 **study**	勉強する study 勉強ができる［できない］ be good [poor] at studying 　学校の勉強ができなくても、成功した人はたくさんい 　る。There are many successful people who were poor 　at studying in school. 勉強に力を入れる study hard; devote one's time to 　studying 勉強になる learn a lot (from the experience) 　今回の経験は、とてもいい勉強になりました。I have 　learned a lot from this experience. 勉強を見る help someone with their studies 　そのセンターでは、大学生のボランティアが子供たち 　の勉強を見てくれる。College students volunteer to 　help children with their studies at the center.

問題
problem

問題が出る a question is given/comes up
昨日の試験では、予想していた通りの問題が出た。
The questions on yesterday's exam were the same as I had expected.

問題を解く solve a problem
クラスの誰ひとり、その問題を解けなかった。Not a single person in the class could solve the problem.

問題に取り組む tackle a problem

レベル
level

レベルが高い「低い」the level is high [low]
このクラスは、私には少しレベルが高い。The level of this class is a bit too high for me.

レベルが上がる the level improves
その学校はここ数年で学力レベルが上がってきた。
The academic level of the school has been going up over the last few years.

レベルが下がる／落ちる the level gets worse/deteriorates

レベルを上げる raise the level
レベルを下げる／落とす lower the level
あるレベルに達する reach a certain level

論文・レポート
paper

論文を書く write a paper
論文を提出する submit a thesis
なんとか期限までに、論文を提出することができた。I somehow managed to submit my thesis by the deadline.

論文を発表する deliver a treatise; publish a paper
その教授は言語学に関する論文を、いくつも発表しています。The professor has published many papers on linguistics.

Student Life

給食
school lunch

給食が出る school lunch is served
この地域の中学校ではすべて、同じ給食センター

で調理された給食が出る。Lunches made by the same caterer are served in all junior high schools in this area.

給食を食べる eat a school lunch

給食を残す leave one's school lunch unfinished

私が中学のころは、給食を残すと先生に怒られたものだった。When I was in junior high, I was scolded by my teacher if I left my lunch unfinished.

給食当番になる be a school-lunch server

給食費を払う pay for school-lunch expenses

クラブ・サークル(活動)・部活
club activities

クラブに入る join a club

クラスの半数以上の生徒は、何らかのクラブに入っている。More than half of the class belongs to some club.

クラブに勧誘する ask ... to join the club

クラブをサボる skip one's club activities

クラブを辞める quit a club

受験のために、クラブを辞めた生徒が、たくさんいます。A lot of students quit their clubs because they had to prepare for entrance exams.

クラブを掛け持ちする belong to two (or more) clubs

クラブ活動をする do a club activity

校則
school rules

校則を守る obey school rules/regulations

校則に違反する／反する break school rules

髪の毛を染めるのは、校則に違反している。It's against the school rules to have dyed hair.

校則を変える change school rules

生徒たちは学校側を説得して、いくつかの校則を変えた。The students succeeded in persuading the school administration to change some of the rules.

校則に縛られる be bound by school rules

修学旅行
school trip

修学旅行に行く go on a school trip

その高校では、毎年韓国へ修学旅行に行きます。They go on a school trip to South Korea every year.

修学旅行の積立をする save for a school trip

修学旅行を引率する supervise the class on its school trip

修学旅行を中止する cancel a school trip

目的地の一つで大きな地震があったため、今年の修学旅行は中止された。A big earthquake occurred in one of the school trip destinations, so the trip was canceled this year.

文化祭
school festival

文化祭の準備をする prepare for a school festival

文化祭の準備をするため、大勢の生徒が遅くまで学校に残っている。Many students stay late at school to prepare for the school festival.

文化祭で模擬店を出す operate a (refreshment) booth at a school festival

文化祭を開催する hold a school festival

我が校では例年通り、１１月３日と４日に文化祭を開催します。We will hold the school festival on November 3 and 4 as usual.

文化祭を中止する cancel a school festival

文化祭のイベントを企画する plan events for a school festival

Job Hunting

機会
chance,
opportunity

機会がある have a chance/an opportunity

日本で長く翻訳の仕事をしている人に、話を聞く機会があった。I had a chance to talk with a person who has worked for a long time as a translator in Japan.

機会がない have no occasions

会社では、なかなか日本人と知り合う機会がない。We have few chances to get to know Japanese people at work.

機会を得る get a chance

機会を失う lose a chance

機会を逃す miss an opportunity

そんなにいい機会を逃すなんて、もったいないことをしたね。It's a shame that you missed such a great opportunity.

機会に恵まれる be given an opportunity
その会社の業務を、1か月ほど体験する機会に恵まれた。I was given an opportunity to work at that company for a month on a trial basis.

機会を与える give someone a chance
お目にかかる機会を与えていただき、感謝しております。I'm grateful that you have given me the chance to see you.

経験
experience

経験がある［ない］have some [no] experience
私は3年間、高校で英語を教えた経験があります。I have three years' experience in teaching English at high schools.

経験を生かす make use of one's experience
彼は俳優の経験を生かして、遊園地での仕事を得た。He made use of his experience as an actor and got a job at an amusement park.

経験を積む gain/accumulate experience
経験済みだ have experience in ...

資格
license,
qualification

資格を持っている have a license/qualification
私は、カリフォルニア州の弁護士の資格を持っています。I have a license to practice law in the state of California.

資格を取る obtain a license
資格を生かす make use of one's license
会計士としての資格を生かせる仕事を探しています。I'm looking for a job in which I can make use of my license in accounting.

仕事
job, work

仕事を探す look for a job
仕事を見つける find a job
英会話学校の講師の仕事を見つけた。I found a job as an instructor at an English conversation school.
仕事(を)する work

仕事を楽しむ enjoy one's work
　この会社の社員はみんな、仕事を楽しんでいるように見える。The staff members of this company seem to be enjoying their work.

仕事を続ける continue one's career
　これからも、翻訳の仕事は続けていきたいと思います。I'd like to continue my career as a translator.

仕事を辞める quit one's job

仕事がはかどる make progress with/in one's work
　今日はかなり仕事がはかどったので、早く帰れそうだ。I've made a lot of progress with my work today, so I'll be able to go home early.

仕事がない／休みだ be off
　明日は仕事がないから、どこか遊びに行こうか。I'm off tomorrow, so shall we go somewhere?

仕事がたまっている have a lot of work left undone

仕事に打ち込む devote/dedicate oneself to work

仕事が行き詰まる be bogged down with/at work

仕事をもらう undertake a job; be given a job

仕事で出張する go on a business trip

仕事に手をつける get down to work; start to work; set out to work

仕事に追われる be very busy with work; be pressed by work

仕事を（1日）休む take (a day) off

仕事の手を休める take a break from work

就職
employment

就職する find employment; get a job

就職口を見つける find a job
　中国の貿易会社に就職口を見つけました。I found a job at a trading company in China.

就職活動をする go job hunting
　2年のイギリス留学を終えて帰国し、就職活動をしています。I came back from Britain after studying there for two years, and now I'm looking for a job.

就職難だ it is hard to get a job

<ruby>人材<rt>じんざい</rt></ruby>
human resources

<ruby>人材<rt>じんざい</rt></ruby>を<ruby>探<rt>さが</rt></ruby>す look for capable people

<ruby>人材<rt>じんざい</rt></ruby>がそろっている have an efficient staff

この<ruby>会社<rt>かいしゃ</rt></ruby>には、とても<ruby>優秀<rt>ゆうしゅう</rt></ruby>な<ruby>人材<rt>じんざい</rt></ruby>がそろっている。
This company has a very efficient staff.

<ruby>人材<rt>じんざい</rt></ruby>を<ruby>育成<rt>いくせい</rt></ruby>する develop/train human resources

<ruby>人材<rt>じんざい</rt></ruby>を<ruby>活用<rt>かつよう</rt></ruby>する make use of human resources

<ruby>人材<rt>じんざい</rt></ruby>を<ruby>派遣<rt>はけん</rt></ruby>する dispatch temporary staff

<ruby>人材<rt>じんざい</rt></ruby>を<ruby>集<rt>あつ</rt></ruby>める recruit staff

<ruby>面接<rt>めんせつ</rt></ruby>
interview

<ruby>面接<rt>めんせつ</rt></ruby>を<ruby>受<rt>う</rt></ruby>ける have an interview

<ruby>先週<rt>せんしゅう</rt></ruby>、<ruby>社長<rt>しゃちょう</rt></ruby>と<ruby>人事<rt>じんじ</rt></ruby><ruby>部長<rt>ぶちょう</rt></ruby>の<ruby>面接<rt>めんせつ</rt></ruby>を<ruby>受<rt>う</rt></ruby>けた。I had an interview with the president and personnel manager last week.

<ruby>面接<rt>めんせつ</rt></ruby>する interview

<ruby>面接<rt>めんせつ</rt></ruby>に<ruby>通<rt>とお</rt></ruby>る be employed after passing an interview

<ruby>面接<rt>めんせつ</rt></ruby>に<ruby>通<rt>とお</rt></ruby>って<ruby>採用<rt>さいよう</rt></ruby>になったと、<ruby>会社<rt>かいしゃ</rt></ruby>から<ruby>電話<rt>でんわ</rt></ruby>で<ruby>連絡<rt>れんらく</rt></ruby>があった。I got a call from the company saying that I have been accepted after passing the interview.

<ruby>面接<rt>めんせつ</rt></ruby>で<ruby>緊張<rt>きんちょう</rt></ruby>する／あがる get nervous at an interview

<ruby>面接<rt>めんせつ</rt></ruby>で<ruby>落<rt>お</rt></ruby>とされる be rejected (as a candidate) after an interview

<ruby>履歴書<rt>りれきしょ</rt></ruby>
résumé

<ruby>履歴書<rt>りれきしょ</rt></ruby>を<ruby>書<rt>か</rt></ruby>く write a résumé

<ruby>履歴書<rt>りれきしょ</rt></ruby>を<ruby>出<rt>だ</rt></ruby>す submit a résumé

<ruby>5<rt>ご</rt></ruby><ruby>社<rt>しゃ</rt></ruby>に<ruby>履歴書<rt>りれきしょ</rt></ruby>を<ruby>出<rt>で</rt></ruby>して、うち<ruby>2<rt>に</rt></ruby><ruby>社<rt>しゃ</rt></ruby>から<ruby>面接<rt>めんせつ</rt></ruby>に<ruby>呼<rt>よ</rt></ruby>ばれた。I submitted a résumé to five companies and two of them asked me to come for an interview.

<ruby>履歴書<rt>りれきしょ</rt></ruby>を<ruby>返送<rt>へんそう</rt></ruby>してもらう have one's résumé returned

Pay & Benefits

<ruby>給料<rt>きゅうりょう</rt></ruby>
pay

<ruby>給料<rt>きゅうりょう</rt></ruby>をもらう get one's pay

<ruby>給料<rt>きゅうりょう</rt></ruby>が<ruby>出<rt>で</rt></ruby>る get paid

<ruby>昨日<rt>きのう</rt></ruby><ruby>給料<rt>きゅうりょう</rt></ruby>が<ruby>出<rt>で</rt></ruby>たから、<ruby>今日<rt>きょう</rt></ruby>はおごってあげるよ。I'll treat today since I got paid yesterday.

<ruby>給料<rt>きゅうりょう</rt></ruby>が<ruby>上<rt>あ</rt></ruby>がる［<ruby>下<rt>さ</rt></ruby>がる］one's salary increases [decreases]

去年に比べて、給料がかなり上がった。My salary increased quite a bit compared with last year's.

給料が減る one's pay is reduced

給料が安い／少ない the pay is bad/low

この会社は給料が安いので、転職を考えています。 The pay is low at this company, so I'm thinking of changing jobs.

給料が高い the pay is good

給料を払う／支払う pay someone's salary

給料がいい［悪い］the salary is good [bad]

その仕事はかなりきついけれど、給料はいい。The job is pretty hard, but you can earn a good salary.

税金
tax

税金を払う pay taxes

税金が引かれる／差し引かれる tax is deducted

報酬から10％の税金が引かれます。Ten percent tax is deducted from the fee.

税金が返ってくる taxes are refunded

確定申告をすると、いくらか税金が返ってくる。 Some taxes will be refunded if you file your final income tax return.

税金がかかる tax is imposed; be taxed

たばこには高い税金がかかっている。Tobacco is heavily taxed.

税金を滞納する be in arrears with one's taxes

税金を納める pay taxes

ボーナス
bonus

ボーナスが出る a bonus is paid

不況のため、ここ数年はボーナスが出ていない。Due to the recession, we haven't received bonuses for the last few years.

ボーナスが減る a bonus is reduced

ボーナスがカットされる a bonus is reduced; a bonus is not paid

今年のボーナスは２０％カットされる。The bonus this year will be reduced by 20 percent.

ボーナスをもらう get a bonus

有(給)休(暇)・休暇 ゆう きゅうきゅう か きゅうか **vacation**	有休を取る take time off with pay ゆうきゅう と 1週間有休を取って、沖縄に行ってきました。I took いっしゅうかんゆうきゅう と おきなわ い a week off and went to Okinawa. 有休を消化する use up one's paid vacation time ゆうきゅう しょうか 有休を使う take one's paid vacation ゆうきゅう つか 仕事が忙しくて、なかなか有休を使うことができ しごと いそが ゆうきゅう つか ない。I've been so busy that I can hardly take my paid vacation.

Employment Status

(アル)バイト **part-time(er)**	アルバイトをする do a part-time job 夜はバーテンのアルバイトをしています。I work よる part-time as a bartender at night. アルバイトを探す look for a part-time job さが アルバイトを募集する look for a part-time employee ぼしゅう 土日に働いてもらえるアルバイトを募集していま どにち はたら ぼしゅう す。We are looking for a part-time employee who can work on weekends. アルバイトを見つける find a part-time job み アルバイトを雇う employ a part-time worker やと そのファーストフード店では、高校生のアルバイ てん こうこうせい トをたくさん雇っている。That fast-food restaurant やと employs a lot of high school students as part-time workers.
(正/契約/派遣) せい けいやく はけん **社員** しゃいん **(regular/contract/temporary)** **employee**	(正)社員になる become a regular employee; become せい しゃいん employed 最初の2年は契約社員でしたが、その後正社員に さいしょ にねん けいやくしゃいん ご せいしゃいん なりました。I was a contract employee for the first two years, and then became a regular employee. 社員を雇う hire/employ some people しゃいん やと 社員を募集する seek a full-time employee; look for a しゃいん ぼしゅう full-timer 社員をリストラする dismiss/fire an employee as part しゃいん

of restructuring

うちの会社でも、いよいよ社員をリストラせざるをえなくなった。Our company is now forced to fire some employees as part of restructuring.

社員を解雇する／首にする dismiss/fire an employee

パート（タイム）
part-time(er)

パートをする do a part-time job

パートで働く work part-time

スーパーのレジ係の多くは、パートで働く主婦です。Most of the cashiers at supermarkets are housewives working part-time.

パートを雇う hire a part-timer

パートを解雇する／切る fire a part-timer

その工場は来月、100人ものパートを解雇すると、発表した。The factory announced that it would fire as many as 100 part-time workers in the next month.

フリー（ランス）
freelance(er)

フリーで働く work freelance

去年の10月に会社を辞めて、それ以来フリーで働いています。I left the company last October, and I've been working freelance ever since.

フリーになる go freelance

フリーの…を雇う／使う hire a freelance ...

今回は、フリーのカメラマンを使うことになった。We decided to hire a freelance photographer this time.

Office Life

営業
business, sales

営業で回る go from place to place on business

彼はいつも営業で外を回っていて、社内にいることはほとんどない。He is always out on business and is hardly ever in the office.

営業を始める open for business; open up a new business

そのレストランは、明日から営業を始めるようだ。

It looks like the restaurant will open tomorrow.

営業は終了している business is closed (for today)

営業戦略を立てる plan a marketing strategy

会議・打ち合わせ meeting

会議に出る attend a meeting

鈴木さんは会議に出ていて、席にいなかった。

Mr. Suzuki was away from his desk at a meeting.

会議に出席する attend a meeting

会議に出席したほぼ全員が、その企画に反対した。

Almost everyone at the meeting opposed the plan.

会議を欠席する miss a meeting

会議を延期する put off/postpone a meeting

社長のスケジュールの都合で、会議は延期された。

The meeting was postponed because of the president's schedule.

会議を始める begin a meeting

会議が終わる the meeting is over

会議を開く hold/have a meeting

明日、新製品の営業戦略に関する会議を開きます。

We will have a meeting tomorrow to plan the marketing strategy for our new product.

会議を予定する arrange a meeting

会議を終了する conclude a meeting

会議に諮る bring up (an issue, etc.) at a meeting

会議を招集する call a meeting

会社・職場・事務所 company, workplace, office

会社に就職する be hired by a company

会社に入る start working at a company

大学を卒業してすぐ、おもちゃを作る会社に入りました。 I started working at a toy manufacturer right after graduating from college.

会社に勤める work for a company

彼は30年ずっとこの会社に勤めている。 He's been working for this company for 30 years.

会社を首になる be fired (from one's job)

会社を辞める leave the company; quit one's job

来年会社を辞めて、自分で事業を起こそうと思っ

ています。I'm thinking of leaving the company and starting my own business next year.

会社が倒産する a company goes bankrupt

会社を経営する manage/run a company

会社を経営するというのは、私には向いていない。
I'm not fit for managing a company.

会社を設立する set up/start/establish a company

会社をサボる skip work

こんなにいい天気の日には、会社をサボって遊びに行きたいなあ。I want to skip work and go outside on such a beautiful day like this.

会社を休む do not go to work

インフルエンザで会社を1週間休んでしまった。I couldn't go to work for a week due to the flu.

会社を（定年）退職する retire from one's company

機械・マシン
machine

機械を操作する operate a machine

この機械を操作するには、特別の資格がいる。You need to be qualified to operate this machine.

機械に詳しい／強い be familiar with machinery

彼は機械に詳しいから、何か困ったことがあったら彼に聞きなさい。He's familiar with the machinery, so ask him if you have any troubles.

機械に疎い／弱い be unfamiliar with machinery

機械を修理する／直す repair a machine

機械を始動させる start a machine

機械を停止させる／止める shut down/turn off/stop a machine

機械が動かない a machine doesn't work

突然機械が動かなくなって、作業がストップした。
The machine suddenly stopped working properly and the work was suspended.

機械を組み立てる set up/assemble a machine

機械を据え付ける install a machine

技術
technology

技術を身につける acquire a skill

技術を習得する master a skill

その技術を習得するには、長い年月がかかる。It takes a long time to master that skill.

技術を磨く improve one's skills

彼らは互いに競い合って、技術を磨いています。They are competing with each other to improve their skills.

技術を開発する develop a (new) technology

この技術を開発したのは、ある小さな町工場の職人です。A worker at a small factory developed this technology.

技術を要する require technique

技術が進歩する technology advances

首
dismissal,
the boot

首が危ない one's job may be at stake

営業部長は、いよいよ首が危ないとのうわさだ。The rumor is that the sales manager could be fired at any time now.

首が飛ぶ be fired; get the ax

彼は今度の仕事で致命的な失敗をしたら、首が飛ぶだろう。He will get the ax if he makes a fatal mistake in the next project.

首がつながる avoid getting fired

首を切る dismiss; fire

計画
plan

計画する plan; make plans

計画を立てる make plans

その会社は新たに、大阪に2店舗出店する計画を立てている。They are planning to launch two shops in Osaka.

計画を実行する carry out a plan

計画がポシャる a plan ends in failure

この計画がポシャると、彼はほかの部署に飛ばされるかもしれない。If this plan ends in failure, he might be demoted to another department.

計画がうまくいく a plan works out

計画が狂う a plan derails

計画を練る work out a plan

計画を見直す review a plan

社内で反対が強かったため、その計画を見直すこと

になった。There was strong opposition within the

company, so the plan is going to be reviewed.

計画を断念する give up a plan

厳しい経済状況のために、その計画を断念せざる

をえなかった。We had to give up the plan due to the

severe economic situation.

計画に賛成する approve a plan

この計画に賛成の人は、手を挙げてください。Those

who approve this plan, please raise your hand.

計画に反対する disapprove a plan

経費
expenses, cost

経費で落とす claim ... as a deductible expense

これらの本の代金は、経費で落とすことができます。

You can claim the cost of these books as a deduct-

ible expense.

経費を切り詰める cut down on expenses

その会社では、経費を切り詰めるために、ありとあら

ゆる努力をしている。That company is making every

effort to cut down on expenses.

経費を削減する cut expenses

経費がかかる cost

そのイベントは、経費がかかりすぎるという理由で、

取りやめになった。The event was canceled because

it cost too much.

経費がかさむ cost much

コピー
copy

コピーをとる copy; make a copy

企画書を提出する前に、コピーをとっておくのを

忘れないように。Don't forget to make a copy of the

proposal before submitting it.

コピーを頼む ask someone to make a copy

コピー(機)の操作を間違える incorrectly operate a

photocopier

コピーの操作を間違えて、紙を200枚も無駄にし

てしまった。I made a mistake operating the photocopier and wasted as many as 200 pieces of paper.

コピー（機）のトナーが切れる the photocopier toner runs out

コピーの紙が足りない be short of (photocopier) paper

作業
work

作業をこなす do the work

作業を進める carry out the work

作業を進めていく上で、いくつか質問したいことが出てきました。 As I carried out the work, a few questions came up that I would like to ask.

作業を担当する take charge of a job; do the work

作業を分担する share the work

何人かで作業を分担しないと、納期に間に合わないだろう。 Unless we share the work among several people, we won't finish it by the due date.

作業にかかる start working; get down to work

データを受け取りしだい、作業にかかります。 I'll get down to work as soon as I receive the data.

条件
condition,
term

条件がある have a condition; there are some conditions

条件を付ける make/set a condition

条件を受け入れる accept someone's terms

彼らは、こちらが提示した条件をすべて受け入れた。 They accepted all the terms we offered.

条件に合う meet someone's requirements

ようやく条件に合う人が見つかった。 We finally found a person who met our requirements.

条件に恵まれている enjoy favorable conditions

条件を飲む reluctantly accept someone's terms

今回だけは、そちらの条件を飲んで、その仕事を引き受けます。 We agree to take on the job on your terms this time only.

条件を満たす meet requirements

いくつかの条件を満たさないと、その仕事には応募できない。 You must meet some requirements in order to apply for the job.

（…を）条件とする be conditional on ...

情報
information

情報を集める gather/collect information

その会社に関する情報を、できるだけたくさん集めてください。 Collect as much information as possible about the company.

情報を漏らす leak information

どんな理由であっても、顧客の情報を漏らすことは固く禁じられています。 Leaking clients' information for any reason is strictly prohibited.

情報を処理する process data

情報を交換する exchange information

情報を提供する offer/provide information

書類
documents

書類を作成する draw up a document

私の仕事には、役所に提出する書類を作成することも含まれます。 My work includes drawing up documents to submit to the government.

書類をまとめる put documents together

書類を提出する submit documents/papers

書類選考をする screen applications

書類選考をして、10名の応募者に絞り、面接に呼んだ。 We screened the applications to narrow down the applicants to 10, and then called them for an interview.

資料
materials

資料をまとめる put material together

資料を準備する prepare material

明日の会議の資料を準備しなければならないので、今日は残業だ。 I'll have to work overtime today because I have to prepare material for tomorrow's meeting.

資料に目を通す skim through the material

会議の前に、ざっと資料に目を通しておくように。 Skim through the material before the meeting.

資料を集める collect/gather material

進歩
progress

進歩を遂げる make progress

省エネ技術はここ10年の間に大きな進歩を遂げた。 Energy-saving technology has progressed remarkably over the last decade.

進歩を妨げる obstruct progress

進歩についていく keep up with the progress/advances

　もともと機械は苦手なので、最近のパソコンの進歩にはついていけない。I can't keep up with the advances in computers as I don't care for them from the start.

進歩が見られる show signs of progress/improvement

スケジュール
schedule

スケジュールを調整する arrange one's schedule

　スケジュールを調整して、その会議には必ず出るようにしてください。Make sure to arrange your schedule and attend the meeting.

スケジュールを変更する reschedule

スケジュールが詰まっている have a tight schedule

　来週はスケジュールが詰まっていて、あなたに会う時間が取れません。I have a tight schedule next week, so I won't be able to see you.

スケジュールがきつい one's schedule is very tight/full

スケジュールを立てる make (out)/plan a schedule

　そのプロジェクト全体のスケジュールを立ててください。Please make an overall schedule for the project.

席
seat

席を外す leave (one's desk)

　急用で1時間ほど席を外します。I'll be out for about an hour on urgent business.

席を外している be not at one's desk

　申し訳ありませんが、彼は今、席を外しています。I'm sorry, but he is not at his desk now.

席を離れる leave one's seat

席を立つ stand up from one's seat; leave one's seat

席に戻る go back to one's seat

席を設ける hold/arrange a meeting/party

　会議の後に、関係者全員の親睦を深めるための席を設けてあります。We have arranged a party for everyone involved to get acquainted.

席に着く take one's seat; be seated

設備
equipment

席を勧める offer someone a seat

設備がいい［悪い］ be well [badly] equipped

設備が整っている be equipped with many facilities

この研究所は政府の援助を受けているので、最新の設備が整っている。 This laboratory has received financial support from the government, so it has all the newest facilities.

設備が不十分だ be not fully equipped

設備を新しくする modernize equipment

すべての工場の設備を新しくするには、かなりのコストと時間がかかる。 It will cost a lot and take considerable time to modernize equipment at all the factories.

(…の)設備がある be equipped with ...

この部屋には暖房の設備がある。 This room is equipped with a heater.

データ
data

データを入力する input data

データをチェックする check the data

データを(間違って)消す delete the data (by mistake)

そのデータを間違って消してしまったときは、心臓がとまるかと思った。 I almost had a heart attack when I deleted the data by mistake.

データを分析する analyze data

データを集める gather data

データが流出する data is leaked

その保険会社の約1万人分の顧客データが、流出した。 Data for about 10,000 of the insurance company's clients was leaked.

データを保存する save data

データをやり取りする exchange data

大容量のデータをやり取りするとき、メールではうまく送れないときがある。 When we exchange large amounts of data, we sometimes can't send it properly by e-mail.

パソコン **personal computer**	パソコンが固まる a computer screen freezes どうしたわけか、1時間に1回はパソコンが固まる。 I don't know why, but the computer screen freezes once every hour. パソコンがハングアップする／フリーズする a computer screen freezes パソコンを起動させる boot up a computer パソコンを修理に出す send one's computer out for repairs 今パソコンを修理に出しているので、急ぎの仕事はお受けできません。I can't take on any urgent jobs because I have sent my computer out for repairs. パソコンを立ち上げる boot up a computer 最近はパソコンを立ち上げるのに、10分以上かかる。It takes more than 10 minutes to boot up my computer these days. パソコンを強制終了する forcibly shut down a computer
はんこ・判 **seal**	はんこを押す stamp with one's seal はんこをもらう receive a stamped seal 書類に必要事項を書いたら、上司のはんこをもらって経理に提出してください。Once you have filled out the form, have it stamped with your boss's seal, then submit it to accounting. はんこを作る make a seal
ファックス **fax**	ファックスを送る send a fax ファックスで送る send by fax 修正の入ったページだけ、ファックスでお送りいただけますか? Could you send only the pages that have been corrected by fax? ファックスを受け取る receive/get a fax ファックスが届く receive a fax; a fax arrives
プレゼン （テーション） **presentation**	プレゼンをする give/make a presentation プレゼンの準備をする prepare for a presentation プレゼンを成功させる make a successful presentation

プレゼンを成功させるためには、周到な準備が必要だ。 You have to meticulously prepare to make a successful presentation.

プログラム
program

プログラムを作る make a (computer) program
主にゲームソフトのプログラムを作ってきました。 I have made programs mainly for video game software.

プログラムを組む arrange a program
プログラムを書く write a (computer) program
プログラムを実行する run a program
そのプログラムを実行したら、固まってしまった。
I ran the program, and then the screen froze.

報告(書)
report

報告(書)を書く write/draw up a report
来週月曜までに、研修の報告書を書いて提出しなければならない。 I have to write a report on the training and submit it by next Monday.

報告(書)をまとめる make a report
報告(書)を提出する submit a report
報告書に目を通す browse through a report
上司は私の報告書にざっと目を通し、すぐに書き直すよう言った。 My boss browsed through my report and then told me to rewrite it right away.

報告書を作成する write/draw up a report

店
store

店を出す open a store
彼女は自宅のそばに、手作りのパンとケーキの店を出した。 She opened a store that sells homemade bread and cakes near her house.

店を経営する run/operate a store
店をたたむ close down a store
2年間飲食店をやっていましたが、去年店をたたんで故郷に戻ってきました。 I ran a restaurant for two years, but closed it down last year and came back to my hometown.

店で働く work at a store
店を手伝う help out at a store

忙しいときは、友人が来て店を手伝ってくれます。

When we get really busy, a friend comes and helps us out at the store.

店を改装する remodel/refurbish a store

店を広げる／拡張する expand a store

店を開ける［閉める］open [close] a store

見積もり
estimate, quote

見積もりをする make an estimate

見積もりを出す submit an estimate

以下の作業について、見積もりを出していただけますか？ Could you give us a quote for the job described below?

見積もりを依頼する ask ... to make an estimate; ask for a quotation

見積もりを取る get a quotation

その仕事について、4社から見積もりを取った。

We have received quotes for the job from four companies.

名刺
business card

名刺を配る give out one's business cards

名刺を交換する exchange business cards

パーティーの前半は、名刺を交換することに終始した。

We continued exchanging business cards during the first half of the party.

名刺を渡す give one's business card

名刺を作る make business cards

彼は仕事用とプライベート用の、2種類の名刺を作っている。 He has prepared two kinds of name cards, one for business and the other for private use.

命令
order, command

命令する order; command

命令に従う obey/follow an order

彼は上司の命令には、いつも黙って従う。 He always follows his boss's orders without making any objections.

命令にそむく disobey an order

命令を下す give an order

命令を出す give an order

本社から、中国での事業中止の命令が出された。
We were given the order from the head office to stop doing business in China.

メール
e-mail

メールをチェックする check e-mail
朝出社すると、まずコーヒーを入れてメールをチェックします。When I come to the office in the morning, I make coffee and then check my e-mail.

メールを送る／出す／送信する send an e-mail
問い合わせ用のアドレスにメールを出したが、まだ返事が来ない。I sent an e-mail to the contact address but haven't gotten a reply.

メールを受け取る／もらう／受信する get/receive an e-mail

メールに返信する reply to an e-mail
毎日数十通のメールに返信するだけでも、かなりの時間がかかる。It takes a lot of time just to reply to the dozens of e-mails I get every day.

メールに添付する attach to an e-mail

メールが来る／着く get an e-mail

メモ
memo

メモ(を)する take/make a note

メモを取る take/make notes
彼女は会議中、頻繁にメモを取る。She often takes notes during meetings.

メモを渡す hand someone a note; slip someone a note

メモを残す leave a message
机の上にメモを残しておきますので、戻ってきたらごらんください。I'll leave a message for you on your desk, so please look at it when you come back.

目標
objective, goal

目標を立てる set one's goal
スタッフ全員が、それぞれの目標を立ててがんばっています。Each employee has set his or her own goal and is working hard.

目標を達成する achieve one's goal
前期の売り上げ目標を、無事達成することができた。We successfully achieved our sales target for

the first half of the year.

目標を見失う lose sight of one's goal

目標にする have/set ... as one's goal

日本語能力試験の1級に合格することを、目標にしています。I am aiming to pass the first grade of the Japanese Language Proficiency Test.

予定
plan, schedule

予定を立てる make plans

予定を組む make plans; make a schedule

予定を変更する change one's schedule

2時から会議となっていましたが、予定を変更して3時半からとします。The meeting was set for two, but we'll change it to three-thirty.

予定が狂う disrupt a schedule

インフルエンザにかかって、仕事の予定が狂ってしまった。I caught the flu, and that totally disrupted my work schedule.

予定に入れる put ... on one's schedule

明日、私との打ち合わせを予定に入れておいてください。Put a meeting with me on your schedule for tomorrow.

予定通りに行う do as scheduled/planned

イベントは台風にもかかわらず、予定通りに行われた。The event was held as planned in spite of the typhoon.

予定がある have plans

予定が詰まっている have a tight/full schedule

利益
profit

利益が出る bring in a profit

小規模の商売では、なかなか利益が出ない。It's difficult for small businesses to bring in a profit.

利益を上げる make/earn a profit

その新製品は幅広い支持を得て、かなりの利益を上げた。The new product became popular and made a large profit.

利益をもたらす return/yield a profit

利益を生む return/yield a profit

利益を生むと思えることには、投資したいと思います。 I want to invest in what I think will yield a profit.

利益になる make a profit

利益を分ける share/allocate the profits

例
example

例にならう follow the example

例を挙げる give an example

少しわかりにくいので、具体的な例を挙げて説明してくれませんか。 It's a bit difficult to understand, so could you give a concrete example and explain?

例が(たくさん)ある there are (many) instances

例がない there is no precedent (for the case)

今までに例がないということで、その会社は私たちの申し出を断った。 They turned down our offer, saying that there was no precedent.

例を示す give an example

(…を)例にとる take ... as an example

連絡
contact

連絡を取る get in touch; contact

連絡がつく be able to reach/contact

さっきから彼の携帯にかけているんだけど、連絡がつかないんだ。 I've been trying to call his cell phone, but I can't reach him.

連絡がある hear from ...

電車が止まっているので遅れると、彼から電話で連絡がありました。 He called and said he would be late because the trains are not in service.

連絡を待つ wait for a call; wait for a reply

では、ご連絡をお待ちしております。 I'll be waiting for your reply.

連絡を取り合う keep in touch

連絡が途絶える lose contact/touch

Special Events

うちあげ
party

うちあげる have a party to celebrate the completion of a project

うちあげをする have a party to celebrate the completion of a project

そのプロジェクトも無事終了したことだし、うちあげをしましょう。Let's have a party now that the project has been completed successfully.

うちあげを企画する plan a party to celebrate

うちあげに出る attend a party to celebrate

金曜は仕事のうちあげに出るから、帰りは遅くなるよ。I'll attend a party to celebrate the completion of a project on Friday, so I'll be home late.

歓迎会・送別会
welcome/ farewell party

歓迎会に出る attend a welcoming party

歓迎会の幹事をやる／務める host a welcoming party

歓迎会の幹事をやることになったんだけど、どこかいい店を知らないかい？ I have to arrange a welcoming party. Do you know any good restaurants?

歓迎会をする／行う hold a welcoming party

今日は、私たちのために歓迎会をしてくださって、どうもありがとうございました。Thank you very much for holding this welcoming party for us today.

歓迎会を企画する plan a welcoming party

歓迎会の準備をする organize a welcoming party

健康診断・人間ドック
medical checkup

健康診断を受ける have a medical checkup

従業員は全員、年に一度健康診断を受ける。All employees get a medical checkup once a year.

健康診断で異常が見つかる some disorders are discovered in one's medical checkup

昇進
promotion

部長に昇進する be promoted to manager

部長に昇進なさったそうで、おめでとうございます。I hear you have been promoted to manager. Congratulations!

昇進が見送られる be passed over for promotion

昇進が早い get a quick promotion

昇進を祝う celebrate someone's promotion

彼の昇進を祝って、ささやかなパーティーを開いた。

We held a small party to celebrate his promotion.

ストレス
stress

ストレスがたまる be under stress

最近は残業も多くて、彼はかなりストレスがたまっているに違いない。He's been working overtime quite often recently, so he must be under a lot of stress.

ストレスになる cause a person stress

ストレスを発散させる get rid of one's stress

あなたはどうやってストレスを発散させていますか？ How do you get rid of your stress?

ストレスを減らす reduce one's stress

ストレスが多い be stressful; give a person a lot of stress

医者というのは、非常にストレスの多い仕事だろう。A doctor's job must be very stressful.

（定年）退職
resignation,
retirement

退職する retire

父は35年勤めた会社を、今日退職する。My father will retire today from the company he has worked at for 35 years.

退職願を出す submit a notice of resignation

彼は1週間ぶりに出社したと思ったら、退職願を出した。He came to the office after a week's absence, and then submitted his notice of resignation.

退職願を受理する accept a notice of resignation

転職
career change

転職する change one's job

彼女は2年間で、8回も転職した。She changed her job as many as eight times over two years.

転職を考えている think of changing one's job

4月に入社した社員のうち、半数以上が転職を考えている。More than half of the employees who joined in April are thinking of changing their jobs.

転職を繰り返す keep changing jobs

リストラ **dismissal** **(due to corpo-** **rate downsizing)**	リストラされる／にあう get fired due to the company's restructuring 彼は去年の10月にリストラされて以来、ずっと仕事を探しているが、まだ見つかっていない。He's been looking for a job since he got fired due to the company's restructuring last October, but hasn't found one. リストラの対象になる be subject to dismissal due to corporate downsizing リストラを断行する carry out company restructuring その会社はリストラを断行し、1年で150人の社員を解雇した。That company carried out restructuring and fired 150 employees in one year.
わいろ **bribe**	わいろを使う use bribery わいろを贈る offer/give a bribe わいろを受け取る receive/accept a bribe 営業部長は、わいろを受け取ったとして、告発された。The sales manager was accused of receiving a bribe. わいろを要求する solicit a bribe わいろが効く a bribe works/is effective

TRAVEL

Streets

横断歩道・踏切
crosswalk,
railroad crossing

横断歩道を渡る cross a crosswalk

自転車に乗ったまま横断歩道を渡ろうとしたら、警官に注意された。 I was warned by a police officer when I crossed the crosswalk on my bike.

横断歩道で止まる stop at a crosswalk

信号がなくても、人が立っていたら、車は横断歩道で止まるべきだ。 Cars should stop at crosswalks when someone is waiting to cross, even if there are no traffic lights.

信号
traffic light

信号で止まる stop at a traffic light

信号が変わる the (traffic) light changes

信号（が変わるの）を待つ／信号待ちをする wait for a light (to change); wait for a green light

信号待ちをしていたら、ばったり友人に会った。 I ran into a friend of mine when I was waiting for the light to change.

信号を無視する ignore a light; run a red light

その車は信号を無視して、猛スピードで走り去った。 The car ran the traffic lights and took off at breakneck speed.

信号を守る observe/obey the traffic lights

一般に、日本人は他の国々の人に比べて、よく信号を守る。 Generally, Japanese people obey traffic lights more than people in other countries do.

道路
road, street

道路を渡る cross a street

道路を渡った反対側に、薬局があります。 There's a drugstore across the street.

道路を横切る cross a street

道路が渋滞する the streets are congested; there is heavy
traffic

夏の間、特に週末には、海へ向かう道路がひどく
渋滞する。During summer, the roads to the beach
get badly congested, especially on weekends.

道路がすいている there is little traffic

連休中、東京では道路がすいていて気持ちがい
い。It's really nice to have so little traffic on the
roads in Tokyo during the long weekend.

歩道
sidewalk

歩道が狭い the sidewalk is narrow

歩道を通る use the sidewalk

歩道を通る場合は、自転車から降りて押して歩くのが
ルールだ。It's a rule that you have to get off your
bike and walk it on the sidewalks.

歩道を歩く walk on/along the sidewalk

(車が)歩道に乗り上げる (a car) drives over a curb and
onto a sidewalk

(車が)歩道に突っ込む (a car) drives onto a sidewalk

その車は歩道に突っ込んで、歩いていた人を二人は
ねた。The car drove onto the sidewalk and hit two
pedestrians.

Trains, Planes & Automobiles

オートバイ・
バイク
motorcycle

オートバイに乗る get on a motorcycle; ride a motorcycle

オートバイを運転する drive/ride a motorcycle

社長は７０歳を超えているが、今でも自分でオー
トバイを運転して会社に来る。The president is over
70, but he still comes to work by motorcycle.

オートバイを乗りこなす handle a motorcycle; control
a motorcycle

そのサーカスでは、オートバイを乗りこなすクマが
人気者だ。The motorcycle-riding bear is a popular

attraction in the circus.

車・自動車
car

オートバイで疾走する drive a motorcycle at full speed

車に乗る get in/into a car; ride in a car

車で行く go by car

渋滞するかもしれないから、車で行くより電車を使ったほうがいい。Maybe you should take a train rather than go by car because the traffic might be heavy.

車で迎えに行く pick someone up

駅に着いたら電話して。車で迎えに行くから。Call me when you get to the station. I'll come and pick you up.

車を運転する drive a car

雪道で車を運転するのには、慣れていない。I'm not accustomed to driving on snowy roads.

車で迎えに来てもらう have someone come pick one up

車に乗せてもらう have someone give one a ride

車で(…まで)送る drive someone somewhere (home, etc.)

偶然その店で隣人に会って、車で家まで送ってもらった。I ran into my neighbor at the store, and he drove me home.

車がエンストする the car stalls

信号待ちをしているときに、車がエンストしてちょっと焦った。I panicked a bit when my car stalled while waiting for the light to change.

車を乗り回す ride around in a car; drive around

車を止める stop a car; pull up a car

車のガソリンが切れる run out of gas

車に同乗する share a car

(座)席
seat

席を取る get a seat (on a train)

自由席の切符しか取れなかったので、早めに並んで席を取らなきゃ。I could only get a ticket for a non-reserved seat, so I'll have to line up early to get a seat.

席を譲る give up one's seat

席を替わる change seats

友人と離れて座っていたら、知らない人が席を替わってくれた。 My friend and I were sitting apart, and then a stranger offered me his seat so that we could sit next to each other.

席を詰める make room (for another to sit down)

席が空いている a seat is vacant

席が空いているかどうか、他の車両を見てこよう。 I'll go and see if there are any (vacant) seats in the other cars.

席が埋まっている／満席だ all seats are occupied/full

自由席／指定席／禁煙席に乗る take a non-reserved seat/a reserved seat/a seat in the non-smoking section

自転車
bike

自転車に乗る get on a bike; ride a bike

自転車で回る ride/cruise/tour around on a bike

1か月かけて、北海道を自転車で回るつもりです。 I'm going to spend a full month touring (around) Hokkaido on my bike.

自転車の二人乗りをする ride double on a bike

自転車を押して歩く walk a bike

坂があまりに急だったので、自転車を降りて押して歩いた。 The slope was so steep I had to get off and walk the bike.

自転車がパンクする get a flat tire

自転車がパンクしたのですが、この近くに修理してもらえるところはありますか？ My bike has a flat tire. Is there a repair shop near here?

自転車で転ぶ fall off a bike

スピード
speed

スピードを上げる speed up

スピードを落とす slow down

電車は駅に近づくにつれて、だんだんスピードを落とした。 The train gradually slowed down as it approached the station.

スピードを出す speed

この通りは交通量が多いので、なかなかスピードが出せない。There's heavy traffic on this street, so you can't go very fast.

(…の)スピードについていく catch up with …

速度
speed

速度が速い［遅い］one's speed is fast [slow]

速度が出る speed

この車は最高でどのくらい速度が出ますか? How fast can this car go?

速度を上げる speed up

速度を落とす slow down

列車は速度を落として、カーブを通過した。The train reduced its speed through the curve.

速度を保つ maintain one's speed

タイヤ
tire

タイヤがパンクする get a flat tire

タイヤを交換する change a tire

ガソリンスタンドでタイヤを交換してもらうと、高くつく。It's rather expensive to have a tire changed at a gas station.

タイヤに空気を入れる pump air into a tire; fill a tire with air

タイヤがすり減る a tire wears down; a tire goes bald

タイヤがすり減っているので、このままだとスリップする危険がある。The tires have worn down, so there is a risk of skidding.

タクシー
taxi, cab

タクシーに乗る get in a taxi; ride in a taxi

タクシーで行く go by taxi; take a taxi

タクシーをつかまえる catch a taxi; hail a cab

バブルのころは金曜の夜などは、なかなかタクシーがつかまらなかった。We could hardly catch a taxi on Friday nights back in the days of the bubble economy.

タクシーを呼ぶ call a taxi

そのショーはかなり遅くまでやっていたので、ホテルに戻るのにタクシーを呼んだ。The show went on until pretty late, so we called a taxi to get back to the hotel.

タクシーを呼び止める get a taxi to stop

タクシーに相乗りする share a taxi

タクシーに相乗りすれば、バスで行くより安い。It's more economical to share a taxi than to go by bus.

タクシーを待たせておく have a taxi wait for one

電車・地下鉄
train, subway

電車に乗る get on a train; ride a train

電車に間に合う catch one's train

早めにホテルを出たので、電車には余裕で間に合った。Since we left the hotel early, we got to the station with plenty of time to catch the train.

電車に乗り遅れる miss one's train

電車を乗り換える change trains; get on another train

その駅で電車を乗り換えるのに、5分しかないからね。We only have five minutes to change trains at that station.

電車が止まっている the train has stopped; the trains have stopped

富山方面への電車は、大雪ですべて止まっています。All the trains going toward Toyama have stopped due to the heavy snow.

電車が遅れている the trains are running late

電車に乗り込む hop on a train

私たちはキオスクでビールとおつまみを買って、電車に乗り込んだ。We bought beer and snacks at the kiosk and hopped on the train.

電車が(ホームに)入る a train enters the station; a train arrives (at the platform)

電車を降りる get off a train

電車が到着する a train arrives

電車が混んでいる［すいている］the train is crowded [not crowded]

電車ががらがらだ the train is almost empty

バス
bus

バスに乗る get on a bus; ride a bus

10番のバスに乗って終点で降りたら、その美術館

は目の前です。Take the No. 10 bus and get off at the last stop, and you'll be in front of the art museum.

バスを降りる get off a bus

バスで行く go by bus; take a bus

旅費を節約するために、東京から京都まで夜行バスで行った。We took a night bus from Tokyo to Kyoto to cut our traveling expenses.

バスを乗り換える change buses; transfer to another bus

バスに乗り込む hop on a bus

バス停で待つ wait at a bus stop

飛行機
plane

飛行機に乗る board an airplane; fly

飛行機に乗り遅れる miss one's plane

その便のアムステルダム到着が2時間遅れたために、ロンドン行きの飛行機に乗り遅れた。The flight to Amsterdam arrived two hours late, so we missed our plane for London.

飛行機が揺れる the plane shakes/rattles

飛行機が嫌いだ hate planes; hate flying

母は飛行機が嫌いで、陸路で行ける所しか旅行しない。My mother hates flying, so she only travels to places you can get to by land.

飛行機に酔う get sick on planes; get airsick

飛行機を乗り継ぐ change planes; make a connection; get a connecting flight

飛行機のキャンセル待ちをする be on a waiting/standby list for a flight

朝から飛行機のキャンセル待ちをして、夕方5時にようやく乗れた。I had been on the waiting list since morning and finally got a seat at five in the evening.

船
boat, ship

船に乗る board a ship

ジュネーブで船に乗って、ローザンヌで降りた。I boarded a ship at Geneva and got off at Lausanne.

船に乗り遅れる miss one's boat

船が揺れる a boat rolls/pitches

船に酔う get seasick; get sick on boats

船が苦手だ don't like boats

私は船が苦手なので、1か月の船旅なんてとても無理だ。I don't like boats, so a one-month cruise is just impossible for me.

船を降りる get off a boat

船で渡る go by boat; cross ... in a boat

Stations

駅
station

駅に着く arrive at the station

駅に着いたら、最終電車がちょうど出たところだった。When I got to the station, the last train had just left.

駅で待ち合わせる wait at the station; meet at the station

明日、10時に駅で待ち合わせましょう。遅れないでね。Let's meet at the station at 10 tomorrow. Don't be late!

駅で会う meet at the station

駅に迎えに行く go to the station to meet someone; go pick someone up at the station

駅に見送りに行く go to the station to see someone off

駅への行き方を聞く ask directions to the station

駅で迷う get lost in a station

駅を乗り越す／乗り過ごす go past one's stop

うとうとしていて、降りる駅を乗り過ごしてしまった。I dozed off and ended up passing my stop.

駅で切符を買う buy a ticket at the station

駅の売店で買う buy ... at a kiosk

駅の階段を駆け上がる run/bound up the stairs in the station

駅のホームで出迎える meet someone on the platform

駅のホームで見送る see someone off on the platform

エスカレーター
escalator

エスカレーターで上がる go up an escalator; take an escalator up (to ...)

エスカレーターで下りる go down an escalator; take an escalator down (to ...)

エスカレーターに乗る ride an escalator; get on an escalator

エスカレーターに乗るときはふつう、急ぐ人のために片側をあけておく。When you get on the escalator, you stand on one side so that those in a hurry can walk up on the other side.

エスカレーターが動く the escalator runs

センサーで人を感知すると、エスカレーターは自動で動きます。When the sensor senses a person, the escalator starts running automatically.

エスカレーターが故障する／止まる the escalator breaks down; the escalator stops

エレベーター
elevator

エレベーターで上がる［下りる］go up [down] in an elevator; take/ride an elevator up [down]

サグラダ・ファミリアの尖塔には、エレベーターで上がることができる。You can go up the spires of the Sagrada Familia by elevator.

エレベーターに乗る get on/in an elevator

エレベーターが故障する／止まる the elevator breaks down; the elevator stops

エレベーターが突然止まり、私を含めて5人が閉じ込められた。The elevator suddenly stopped and five people including me were trapped inside.

改札(口)
turnstile

改札(口)を通る go through a turnstile

改札(口)を出る come out of a turnstile

改札(口)で待ち合わせる meet someone in front of a turnstile (at an agreed time)

明日の2時に、駅の改札で待ち合わせましょう。Let's meet in front of the turnstile at two tomorrow.

改札(口)を間違える go through the wrong turnstile

そのレストランが見つからないと思ったら、改札口を

間違えて駅の反対側に出ていた。I couldn't find the restaurant because I went through the wrong turnstile and came out on the wrong side of the station.

改札が始まっている the ticket gate has opened

階段
stairs

階段を上る［下りる］go up [down] the stairs

膝が痛いので、急な階段を上るのは辛い。With my sore knees, it's tough to go up steep stairs.

階段を駆け上がる［駆け下りる］run/bound up [down] the stairs

大急ぎで駅の階段を駆け上がり、電車に飛び乗った。I bounded up the steps to the platform and jumped into the train.

階段を使う use/take the stairs

階段で行く use/take the stairs

エレベーターが込んでるから、僕は階段で行くよ。I'll use the stairs since the elevator is crowded.

階段を踏み外す slip on the stairs

壁の絵に気を取られて、階段を踏み外してしまった。I was distracted by the painting on the wall, and missed a step and fell down the staircase.

階段から落ちる fall down a staircase/the stairs

Maps & Directions

ガイドブック
guidebook

ガイドブックを持つ carry a guidebook

彼は 10 年前、ガイドブックさえ持たずに日本にやってきた。He came to Japan 10 years ago without even a guidebook.

ガイドブックに載っている be in a guidebook

地元の人に聞けば、ガイドブックには載っていないおいしいお店を教えてもらえるでしょう。Local people can tell you good restaurants that are not in the guidebooks.

ガイドブックで探す look for something in a guidebook

ガイドブックを参考にする refer to a guidebook

時刻表
timetable

時刻表を見る look at a timetable

時刻表を調べる check a timetable

時刻表を調べたら、日が暮れる前には目的地に着けそうだ。I checked the timetable and it looks like we'll get to our destination before dark.

時刻表で確かめる confirm by checking a timetable

時刻表が改正されている the timetable has been revised

地図
map

地図を見る look at a map

地図を見たかぎりでは、その城はそれほど遠くない。As far as I can tell from the map, the castle is not that far away.

地図で調べる look for ... on a map

地図に載っていない be not on a map; doesn't appear on a map

その通りは地図に載っていないかもしれないから、誰かに聞いたほうがいい。You might want to ask someone about the street since it might not be on a map.

地図が読めない be unable to read a map

地図を描く draw a map

彼は、彼の自宅までの地図を描いてくれた。He drew me a map to his house.

道
directions

道を聞く ask for directions

コンビニの店員に、そのホールへの道を聞いた。I asked the clerk at a convenience store for directions to the hall.

道を尋ねる ask for directions

道を間違える take a wrong turn; go down the wrong street; go the wrong way

道に迷う get lost (when trying to follow a map, directions, etc.)

私はひどい方向音痴で、しょっちゅう道に迷う。I have a terrible sense of direction and often get lost.

道が違う go the wrong way; the road one is taking is wrong

ABC ホールに行きたいのですか？　じゃあ道が違いますよ。You want to go to ABC Hall? Then you are going the wrong way.

道が交差している the roads intersect

道が行き止まりだ the road comes to a dead end

道が険しい the path is steep

Airports

空港
airport

空港に着く arrive at an airport

空港に見送りに行く go to an airport to see someone off

空港に迎えに行く go pick someone up at an airport

空港で出迎える greet someone at an airport

インバネス空港では、バグパイプの演奏に出迎えられた。The passengers were welcomed by a bagpipe performance at Inverness Airport.

空港が閉鎖される the airport will close (indefinitely)

空港が混雑する the airport is busy; the airport is bustling with travelers

クリスマスの時期には、たいていどこの空港も混雑する。Almost all the airports are busy around Christmastime.

空港でボディーチェックをされる／受ける undergo a security check; be frisked

最近は、多くの空港で、乗客全員がボディーチェックされる。Recently all the passengers undergo a body check in many airports.

空港で荷物を受け取る receive one's luggage at the airport

空港で荷物を預ける check (in) one's luggage at the airport

空港から宅配で（荷物を）送る send (luggage) by a delivery service from the airport

空港で検疫検査を受ける undergo a quarantine inspection at the airport

出発
departure

出発が遅れる the departure will be delayed

沖縄行きの便は２０分出発が遅れると、アナウンスがあった。There was an announcement that the flight for Okinawa would be delayed 20 minutes.

定刻どおり出発する depart on schedule

この国では、列車が定刻どおりに出発したためしがない。The trains have never run on schedule in this country.

出発時刻に間に合わせる make it in time for departure

出発時刻が迫る the departure time is approaching

税関
customs

税関を通過する go through customs

税関で引っかかる be held up at customs

彼一人が税関で引っかかって、なかなか出てこなかった。He was the only one held up at customs, and it took a long time for him to get through.

税関で没収される have something confiscated by/at customs

税関で押収される have something confiscated by/at customs

大量の麻薬が毎日税関で押収されている。A large quantity of drugs is confiscated by customs every day.

税関で申告する declare ... at customs

今まで一度も、税関で何かを申告したことがありません。I have never once declared ... anything at customs.

税関でパスポートを調べられる one's passport is checked at customs

税関で手荷物／所持品を検査される one's luggage is checked at customs

搭乗口（とうじょうぐち） **boarding gate**	搭乗口に（並んで）待つ wait (in line) at one's board-ing gate 搭乗口へ進む proceed to one's boarding gate 搭乗口へ急ぐ hurry to one's boarding gate 　出発10分前です。搭乗口へお急ぎください。Your flight will leave in 10 minutes. Please hurry to the boarding gate.
到着（とうちゃく） **arrival**	到着が遅れる the arrival will be delayed 到着を待つ wait for someone/something to arrive 　空港ではその俳優の大勢のファンが、今か今かと到着を待っていた。A lot of the actor's fans were anx-iously waiting for him to arrive at the airport. 定刻どおり到着する arrive on time

Itinerary Planning

ツアー **tour**	ツアーに参加する go on a tour; participate in a tour 　そのツアーに参加したのは、多くが退職した年配の夫婦だった。The majority of participants in the tour were retired elderly couples. ツアーに申し込む reserve/book a tour ツアーで回る tour 　私は去年、京都と奈良の有名な寺をツアーで回った。I toured the famous temples in Kyoto and Nara last year.
ホテル・旅館（りょかん） **hotel,** **(Japanese-style)** **inn**	ホテルを予約する reserve/book a hotel ホテル（に部屋）を取る get a room (at a hotel) 　祭りの間は、ホテルを取るのが難しい。It's diffi-cult to get a (hotel) room during the festival. ホテルにチェックインする check in at a hotel 　朝9時にハワイに着いたら、すぐホテルにチェックインすることができます。You can check in at the hotel immediately upon your arrival in Hawaii at nine in the morning.

ホテルをチェックアウトする check out of a hotel

ホテルに滞在する stay at a hotel

ホテルに…泊する stay at a hotel for ... day(s)

　私たちは湖畔のホテルに三泊した。We stayed at a lakeside hotel for three days.

予約
reservation

予約を入れる put in/make a reservation

　帰りの便は、１２月10日に予約を入れた。I booked my return flight on December 10.

予約を取る get/make a reservation

予約を変更する change a reservation

予約をキャンセルする cancel a reservation

　出発の１週間以内にご予約をキャンセルされる場合、５０％のキャンセル料がかかります。If you cancel your reservation within a week of the departure date, you'll be charged a 50 percent cancellation fee.

旅行
trip

旅行に出かける go on a trip

旅行の計画を立てる plan a trip

　実際の旅行よりも、旅行の計画を立てているときのほうが一番楽しい。For me, the best part of a trip is planning it, rather than actually taking it.

旅行を申し込む book a trip/vacation

Sightseeing

案内所
information desk

案内所を探す look for an information desk

　初めての町に着いたら、まず案内所を探します。I always look for an information desk as soon as I arrive somewhere new.

案内所に行く go to an information desk

案内所で尋ねる ask at an information desk

　地元の名物料理が食べられる店を、案内所で尋ねた。I asked at the information desk where I could try the local specialty.

（お）土産
gift, souvenir

（お）土産を見て歩く browse gifts at souvenir shops; look around for gifts

出発までまだ時間があるから、お土産でも見て歩こうか？ We've still got time before our departure, so shall we look around for gifts?

（お）土産を選ぶ choose a gift; decide on a gift to buy

（お）土産を買う buy a gift

（お）土産に…を買う buy ... as a gift/souvenir

私は自分用のお土産に、手編みの手袋を買った。
I bought myself a pair of hand-knitted mittens as a souvenir.

（お）土産を渡す give a gift

（お）土産を頼まれる be asked to buy a gift

海外旅行に行くときは、いつも姪にお土産を頼まれる。Every time I go on a trip abroad, my niece asks me to buy her gifts.

カメラ
camera

カメラを持ち歩く walk around with a camera

彼女は常に一眼レフのカメラを持ち歩いている。
She always carries her SLR camera with her.

カメラで撮る／撮影する capture on camera

カメラを置き忘れる leave one's camera somewhere (unintentionally)

しまった！ タクシーの中にカメラを置き忘れてきた！
Oh no! I left my camera in the taxi!

カメラをなくす lose one's camera

カメラのシャッターを切る snap a shot

カメラに収める capture on camera; get a photo/picture (of ...)

富士山の美しい姿をカメラに収めることができた。
I was able to get a picture of beautiful Mt. Fuji.

写真
photograph

写真を撮る take a picture

（…を）写真に撮る take a picture (of ...)

その黒鳥を写真に撮ろうと、大勢の人が池の周りに集まっていた。A lot of people gathered around the pond trying to take a picture of the black swan.

写真を写す take a picture
写真を撮ってもらう have one's picture taken
　この滝をバックに、写真を撮ってもらおう。Let's have our picture taken with the waterfall in the background.
写真に入る appear in a photograph
　着物を着た日本人女性二人に、一緒に写真に入ってもらった。I asked two Japanese women in kimono to be in a photo with me.
写真を現像する develop photos
写真を引き伸ばす enlarge photos
写真を焼き増しする make more prints of a picture
　この写真を2枚、焼き増ししてもらえますか？ Could you make two more prints of this picture?
写真を送る send a photo
写真がよく撮れている the photo came out well
　あなたがロンドンで撮った写真は、どれもよく撮れていますね。The pictures you took in London all came out well.

Logistics

チケット・乗車券・航空券 ticket, boarding pass

チケットを取る get a ticket
　旅行会社に勤めている友人に、香港までのチケットを取ってもらった。I asked a friend who works for a travel agency to get a ticket to Hong Kong for me.
チケットを予約する reserve a ticket
チケットを払い戻す refund a ticket
　私の乗る便が欠航になったので、チケットを払い戻してもらった。My flight was canceled, so I had my ticket refunded.
チケットをキャンセルする cancel a ticket
チケットを手配する arrange tickets
　オペラのチケットは私が手配してあげるから、心配し

ないように。Don't worry about the opera tickets; I'll arrange them for you.

荷造り
packing

荷造りを頼む ask someone to do the packing (for a trip)

荷造りが出来ている have finished packing

あと1時間で家を出なきゃならないのに、荷造りが全然出来ていない。I'm supposed to leave home in an hour, but I haven't packed anything yet.

荷物
luggage

荷物をまとめる get one's luggage together

10時に出発します。それまでに荷物をまとめておいてください。We'll leave at 10. Please get your belongings ready by then.

荷物を預ける check (in) one's luggage

荷物を駅のコインロッカーに預けて、町を散策した。I put my luggage in a coin locker at the station and took a stroll around town.

荷物を持つ carry luggage

荷物を背負う carry luggage on one's back

荷物になる don't feel like carrying something; be something not worth carrying

そんなにたくさん服を持っていっても、荷物になるだけだよ。Taking that many clothes would just be a burden.

荷物がある have luggage

荷物がたくさんあるので、タクシーで行きます。I have a lot of luggage, so I'm taking a taxi.

荷物を取りにくる come to pick up one's luggage

3時ごろに（荷物を）取りにくるので、それまで預かってもらえませんか？ Could you keep my luggage till I come back to pick it up at around three?

荷物を送り出す send one's luggage

荷物を運ぶ carry luggage

その安ホテルでは、部屋まで自分で荷物を運ばなければならなかった。At the budget hotel I had to carry my luggage to the room myself.

荷物を抱える carry luggage in one's arms

迎え picking someone up	迎えに行く go to pick someone up 迎えに来る come to pick one up; come get one 迎えをよこす send someone to pick someone up 駅に夜 10 時ごろ着くので、誰か迎えをよこしてください。My train will arrive at the station around 10 in the evening, so please send someone to pick me up.
レンタカー rent-a-car	レンタカーを借りる rent a car レンタカーで回る go/drive around in a rent-a-car 沖縄には鉄道がないので、レンタカーで回った。We went around in a rent-a-car in Okinawa since there are no trains there. レンタカーを乗り捨てる drop off a rental car (at a branch different from the one where it was rented) そのレンタカー会社の支店がある町なら、どこでもレンタカーを乗り捨てることができる。You can drop the car off at any of the rental company's branch offices, in any city.

Trouble

スーツケース suitcase	スーツケースがなくなる lose a suitcase 海外旅行で、スーツケースがなくなったことがありますか? Have you ever lost a suitcase on a trip abroad? スーツケースが壊れる a suitcase breaks スーツケースの鍵をなくす lose the key to one's suitcase スーツケースの鍵をなくしたので、壊して開けなければならなかった。I lost the key to my suitcase, so I had to break it open.
盗難 robbery, theft	盗難にあう be robbed そのホテルでは、三人の宿泊客が次々に盗難にあったらしい。I hear that three guests were robbed in quick succession at the hotel.

（警察に）盗難届を出す file a theft report (with the police)

パスポート
passport

パスポートをなくす lose one's passport

パスポートを紛失する lose one's passport

パスポートを盗まれる have one's passport stolen
　財布やトラベラーズチェックと一緒に、パスポートを盗まれた。I had my passport stolen together with my wallet and traveler's checks.

パスポートを忘れる forget (to bring) one's passport
　彼はパスポートを忘れて、予定していた便に乗りそこねた。He forgot to bring his passport and missed his scheduled flight.

パスポートを置き忘れる leave one's passport somewhere (unintentionally)
　パスポートをテーブルの上に置き忘れた。I carelessly left my passport on the table.

パスポートを再発行する reissue a passport

パスポートを偽造する forge a passport

飛行機
plane

飛行機が遅れる the plane will be delayed
　国際便で飛行機が遅れるのは、よくあることだ。It's not unusual for international flights to be delayed.

飛行機が（嵐で）飛ばない the plane has been grounded (due to a storm, etc.)
　もし飛行機が飛ばない場合は、新幹線で広島まで行くつもりだ。If the flight is canceled, I'll take the Shinkansen up to Hiroshima.

飛行機でダブルブッキングされる one's seat is double-booked on a flight

飛行機が満席で乗れない a flight is fully booked and one cannot get a seat

飛行機事故にあう be involved in a plane crash

ENTERTAINMENT

Drinking & Dining Out

お茶
tea

お茶を飲む drink (a cup of) tea
お茶を入れる make tea
　お茶でも入れましょうか? Would you like some tea?
お茶のお代わりをする have another cup of tea
お茶(を)する (go into a café and) have a cup of coffee/
　tea
　スタバでちょっとお茶しようよ。Let's go grab some
　coffee at Starbucks.
お茶に誘う invite someone to tea; ask someone out for
　tea

カフェ・喫茶店
café

カフェに入る go into a café
カフェでひと休みする take a break at a café
　買い物で疲れたので、カフェでひと休みした。I was
　tired from shopping, so I stopped by a café to take a
　break.
カフェでお茶する have a cup of tea at a café
　私たちは、カフェでお茶しながらおしゃべりした。
　We chatted over a cup of tea at a café.
カフェで待ち合わせる meet at a café
喫茶店でおしゃべり(を)する have a chat at a café
喫茶店で本を読む read a book at a café

酒
alcohol, drink

酒を飲む drink alcohol
　私は全くお酒を飲みません。I don't drink at all.
酒が強い can drink a lot
　父はとても酒が強いけど、私は全く飲めない。My fa-
　ther can drink quite a lot, whereas I can't drink at all.
酒が弱い can't drink much

酒が好きだ like drinking alcohol

酒に酔う get drunk

　彼女は酒に酔うと、陽気になる。She's jovial when she's drunk.

酒が回る get drunk

酒が入っている be tipsy

　そのことを彼に相談するなら、酒が入っていないときにしなさい。If you want to talk with him about that, you should do it when he's sober.

酒を断つ／やめる quit drinking

　彼女はその大失態を演じてから、酒を断っています。She quit drinking after she made that awful blunder.

酒を水で割る mix liquor (whiskey, etc.) with water

酒の燗をする heat up/warm up sake

酒を出す serve alcohol

酒を嗜む drink alcohol (moderately)

酒を（一杯）引っかける drink (a glass of beer, etc.); have a drink or two

酒に溺れる indulge in drinking

注文
order

注文（を）する order; make/place an order

　すみません、注文したいのですが。Excuse me, I'd like to order, please.

　チーズバーガーとポテトのSとコーラを注文した。I ordered a cheeseburger, small, french fries, and a cola.

注文を取りにくる come to take an order

　３０分も待っているのに、まだ注文を取りにこない。We've been waiting for 30 minutes and still nobody has come to take our orders.

注文を間違える make a mistake on an order

レストラン・
居酒屋・バー
restaurant,
izakaya, bar

レストランを予約する book a table at a restaurant

　7時に4人で、そのレストランを予約しています。I've reserved a table for four at the restaurant at seven.

レストランに行く go to a restaurant

彼女の誕生日に、フレンチレストランに行った。We went to a French restaurant to celebrate her birthday.

レストランで食べる eat at a restaurant

夕食は、近所のレストランで食べた。I had dinner at a nearby restaurant.

バーをはしごする barhop

Romance

恋人・彼女・彼（氏） boyfriend, girlfriend	恋人がいる have a boyfriend/girlfriend 彼に恋人がいると知ってショックだった。I was shocked to find out he has a girlfriend. 恋人を作る get a boyfriend/girlfriend 日本語が上達する一番いい方法は、日本人の恋人を作ることだ。The best way to improve your Japanese is to get a Japanese boyfriend or girlfriend. 恋人ができる find a boyfriend/girlfriend 恋人と別れる break up with one's boyfriend/girlfriend 恋人にふられる be dumped by one's boyfriend/girlfriend 彼は、3年間付き合った恋人にふられた。His girlfriend dumped him after they were together for three years. 恋人と結婚する marry one's boyfriend/girlfriend
コンパ・合コン party	コンパをする give/have/throw a party コンパを開く give/have/throw a party 来週の金曜日に、クラスのコンパを開きます。We're having a class party on Friday next week. コンパの幹事をする organize a party コンパに行く go to a party
デート date	デート（を）する have a date 私たちは、ディズニーランドでデートした。We had a date at Disneyland. デートに誘う ask someone on a date; ask someone out 彼女をデートに誘ったが、あっさり断られた。She

flatly said no when I asked her out.

デートをすっぽかす stand someone up
彼に初デートをすっぽかされた。He stood me up on our first date.

デートをドタキャンする cancel a date at the last minute
デートの約束をする arrange a date

プロポーズ
proposal

プロポーズ(を)する propose to someone
出会って2か月で、彼にプロポーズされた。He proposed to me two months after we met.

プロポーズを受ける accept someone's proposal (of marriage)

プロポーズを断る turn down someone's proposal (of marriage)
彼女は僕のプロポーズを断って、別の男と結婚した。
She turned down my marriage proposal and got married to another man.

Karaoke

歌・曲
song, tune

歌を歌う sing a song
私はカラオケではいつも、ビヨンセの歌を歌う。I always sing Beyoncé songs at karaoke.

歌を選ぶ choose a song

歌をデュエットする sing a duet
彼とバックストリートボーイズの歌を、デュエットした。
He and I sang a Backstreet Boys song together.

歌をハモる sing in a harmony
彼は合唱部にいたので、どんな歌でもハモってくれる。He used to be in a choir, so he can sing harmony beautifully to any song.

音程
pitch, tune

音程が狂う sing out of tune; sing off-key
彼女の歌は音程が狂っていたが、本人は全然気にしていないようだった。She was singing out of tune, but she didn't seem to care at all.

音程を外す sing out of tune; sing off-key

音程が合っている sing in tune

カラオケ
karaoke

カラオケをする sing at karaoke

カラオケに行く go to karaoke

　仕事の後カラオケに行くんだけど、一緒に行かない？
We're going to karaoke after work. Why don't you come along?

カラオケに誘う ask someone to go to karaoke

カラオケで歌う sing at karaoke

　カラオケで歌いまくると、気分がすっきりする。
Singing a lot of songs at karaoke makes me feel refreshed.

声
voice

声がかれる one's voice gets hoarse

　歌いすぎて、声がかれてしまった。My voice was hoarse from singing too much.

声がかすれる one's voice gets hoarse

声を合わせる sing along

　最後の曲は、みんなで声を合わせて歌った。We all sang along to the last song.

声が(よく)通る one's voice carries well

　舞台俳優として成功するためには、声がよく通ることが重要なポイントだ。In order to succeed as a stage actor, it's important to have a voice that carries well.

声がいい have a good voice

声が出る one's voice can be heard; one's voice is audible

　風邪をひいて声が出ない。I caught a cold and lost my voice.

声を出す make one's voice heard; speak/talk loudly; raise one's voice

　もっと大きな声を出さないと、奥にいる人には聞こえないよ。Raise your voice, or the people in the back won't be able to hear you.

マイク
microphone

マイクを握る hold a microphone

マイクを離さない not let go of a microphone

彼女は一度握ったマイクは、なかなか離さない。She won't let go of the microphone once it's in her hands.

マイクが入っている［いない］a microphone is on [off]

マイクを向ける turn a microphone over to someone

リズム
rhythm

リズムをとる keep rhythm

リズムに乗る get into the rhythm

彼はリズムに乗って体を揺らしながら、大声で歌った。He sang loudly, swaying to the rhythm.

リズムに合わせる adjust to the rhythm

私たちは曲のリズムに合わせて、手拍子をした。We clapped our hands to the rhythm of the music.

リズムが乱れる the rhythm becomes irregular

Movies & Concerts

映画
movie

映画を見る watch a movie

映画はだいたい DVD で見ます。I usually watch movies on DVD.

映画を見に行く go to (see) a movie; go to the movies

今度、映画でも見に行きませんか？ Would you like to go to a movie with me sometime?

1年に3、4回くらい映画を見に行きます。I go to the movies maybe three or four times a year.

映画を見逃す miss a movie

この映画は見逃せない。You can't miss this movie.

映画の前売券を買う buy an advance ticket to a movie

映画を鑑賞する watch a movie

趣味は映画を鑑賞することです。My favorite pastime is watching movies.

コンサート
concert

コンサートに行く go to a concert

来週 AKB 4 8 のコンサートに行きます。I'm going to the AKB48 concert next week.

コンサートがある there will be a concert

8月に東京ドームで、嵐のコンサートがある。Arashi

is giving a concert at Tokyo Dome in August.

コンサートを聴く attend a concert

　サントリーホールで、クラシックのコンサートを聴きました。I attended the symphony at Suntory Hall.

コンサートに招待される be invited to a concert

コンサートに誘われる be asked to go to a concert; be invited to a concert

コンサートのチケットを取る get a concert ticket

チケット
ticket

チケットを買う［売る］buy [sell] a ticket

　最近はインターネットやコンビニで、チケットを買うことができる。Nowadays you can buy tickets online or from convenience stores.

チケットを手に入れる obtain a ticket

　EXILE のチケットを手に入れるのはとても難しい。Exile tickets are very hard to come by.

チケットを予約する book a ticket

チケットが完売する tickets sell out

　明日のライブのチケットは、完売だそうだ。I hear the tickets for tomorrow's show are sold out.

チケットを売り出す put tickets on sale

　イベントのチケットは、土曜日から売り出される。The tickets for the event will go on sale on Saturday.

涙
tears

涙を流す shed tears

涙を浮かべる have tears in one's eyes

　彼は目にうっすらと涙を浮かべていた。He had some tears in his eyes.

涙があふれる break down in tears; burst into tears

涙をこぼす shed tears

涙がこみ上げる tears well up

涙が出る cry; come to tears

涙を見せる cry

　彼女は人前では、決して涙を見せない。She never cries in public.

涙をこらえる／抑える hold back one's tears

涙がかれる one's tears dry up

私は泣いて泣いて、涙がかれるまで泣いた。I cried and cried until my tears dried up.

涙にくれる be in tears

涙にむせぶ be choked with tears

涙を誘う move someone to tears

涙をぬぐう dry/wipe one's tears

拍手
applause

拍手する clap one's hands; applaud

彼女がスピーチを終えると、聴衆全員が拍手をした。The whole audience applauded when she finished her speech.

拍手を送る applaud

拍手で迎える greet someone with applause

彼は盛大な拍手で、ステージに迎えられた。He was greeted with loud applause as he walked on stage.

拍手が起こる applause breaks out

Museums

展覧会
exhibition

展覧会に行く go to an exhibition

近代美術の展覧会に行った。I went to a modern art exhibition.

展覧会が開催される an exhibition is held

人気漫画家の展覧会が、来月開催される。An exhibition by a popular manga artist will be held next month.

展覧会に招待される be invited to an exhibition

展覧会に出品する exhibit one's work at an exhibition

美術館・
博物館
museum

美術館が混んでいる a museum is crowded

美術館はとても混んでいて、絵を全部見るのに4時間かかった。The museum was so crowded that it took me four hours to see all the paintings.

美術館で並ぶ stand in line at a museum

美術館で…を鑑賞する appreciate ... at a museum

美術館巡りをする visit museums

箱根で美術館巡りをして、楽しみました。I had a great time visiting the museums in Hakone.

美術館に展示される／陳列される be exhibited/displayed at a museum

Sports & Outdoor Activities

相手
partner

相手をする play ... with someone

卓球の相手をしてくれる人を探しています。I'm looking for someone to play ping-pong with.

相手にならない be no match for someone

彼女にバドミントンの試合を申し込んだが、私では相手にならなかった。I challenged her to a game of badminton, but I was no match for her.

相手がいる［いない］ have someone [don't have anyone] to play ... with

テニスが好きなんだけど、一緒にする相手がいない。I like tennis, but I don't have anyone to play with.

相手を負かす beat one's opponent

汗
sweat

汗をかく sweat

今日は暑かったので、すごく汗をかいた。It was a hot day, so I sweat a lot.

私は体中に汗をかいていた。I had sweat all over my body.

（ジムで）汗を流す work up a sweat (at a gym)

（シャワーで）汗を流す take a shower to wash off/away the sweat

汗が引く stop sweating

着替えるのは、汗が引くまで待ったほうがいいよ。You should wait to change clothes until after you stop sweating.

汗を抑える decrease sweating

（タオルで）汗を押さえる absorb sweat with a towel

汗をふく wipe off the sweat

彼はタオルで顔の汗をふいた。He wiped the sweat off his face with a towel.

息
breath

息が切れる pant; be out of breath
階段を駆け上がったら、息が切れた。I was out of breath from running up the stairs.

息が上がる pant; be out of breath

息を整える get one's breath back
少し休んで息を整えて、私はまた走り出した。I rested for a while, got my breath back, and started running again.

息を吸う breathe in

息を吐く breathe out

運動
exercise

運動(を)する exercise; do exercise
週に3回、ジムで運動しています。I exercise at a gym three times a week.

運動になる be exercise
階段の昇り降りは、いい運動になる。Walking up and down the stairs is good exercise.

運動不足だ don't get enough exercise
運動不足なので、太ってきた。I've started to gain weight due to lack of exercise.

運動神経がいい［悪い］be athletic [unathletic]; have good [bad] reflexes

温泉
hot spring

温泉に行く go to a hot spring
冬休みは温泉に行って、のんびりする予定です。I'm planning to go to a hot spring and spend time relaxing during my winter vacation.

温泉に入る go into a hot-spring bath

温泉につかる soak in a hot-spring bath
温泉につかって飲む酒は、最高だ。Nothing beats drinking sake in a hot-spring bath.

温泉巡りをする take a tour of hot-springs

温泉で露天風呂に入る go into an open-air/outdoor bath at a hot spring

温泉は…に効く／いい the hot spring is good for ...

ここの温泉は神経痛に効くらしい。They say the hot spring here is good for neuralgia.

体 からだ
body

体を鍛える build oneself up; strengthen one's body

次の東京マラソンに出場するために、体を鍛えています。I'm training to participate in the next Tokyo Marathon.

体を絞る lose weight (by working out)

体にいい［悪い］ be good [bad] for one's health

山のさわやかな空気は、体にいい。Fresh mountain air is good for your health.

体で覚える learn ... by practicing it

スポーツは体で覚えるのが、一番だ。The best way to learn a sport is by practicing it.

体を壊す destroy/ruin one's health

体がもたない can't stay healthy

最低8時間は寝ないと、体がもたない。I'm a wreck if I don't get at least eight hours of sleep.

体が弱る one becomes weak

体の調子がいい［悪い］ be in good [bad] health

キャンプ
camp(ing)

キャンプに行く go camping

今年の夏は、友達と海へキャンプに行った。This summer my friends and I went camping at the seaside.

キャンプ（を）する camp

キャンプでバーベキューをする have a barbecue at a camp

筋肉 きんにく
muscle

筋肉をつける develop muscles

全身にくまなく筋肉をつけるには、とても時間がかかる。It takes a lot of time to develop all the muscles in your body.

筋肉を鍛える strengthen/build up one's muscles

筋肉をほぐす loosen up one's muscles

筋肉が衰える one's muscles become weaker

筋肉を傷める pull a muscle

筋肉が落ちる lose one's muscles

1か月ギプスをしていたら、左脚の筋肉が落ちて

しまった。I've lost a lot of muscle in my left leg because it was in a plaster cast for a month.

試合
game, match

試合をする　play a game/match

彼女とテニスの試合をしたら、強くてびっくりした。I played a tennis match with her and was surprised at how strong she was.

試合に勝つ　win a game/match

全試合に勝つことが、われわれの目標だ。Our goal is to win every game we play.

試合に負ける　lose a game/match

試合で引き分ける　draw a game/match

試合が行われる　a game/match is played

ドイツとアルゼンチンの試合は、明日行われる。The game between Germany and Argentina will be played tomorrow.

試合の応援をする　cheer during a game/match

韓国で行われる日本代表の試合の応援をしに行くために、何日か休みを取った。I took a few days off to go and support the Japanese team in the game played in South Korea.

勝負
game, match

勝負をする　play a game/match

勝負に出る　take a certain action to succeed

そのハンバーガー店は、1個1,000円の高級バーガーで勝負に出た。That hamburger shop went all out to ensure the success of its 1,000-yen deluxe hamburger.

勝負に勝つ　win a game/match

勝負に負ける　lose a game/match

勝負がつく　a game/match is over

挑戦者の右フックでチャンピオンがダウンし、一瞬で勝負はついた。The match was over in a flash as the challenger's right hook knocked out the champion.

勝負を捨てる／投げる　give up a game/match

勝負を挑む　challenge

勝負にならない　be no match

あんな弱いやつが相手じゃ、勝負にならないよ。

He's so weak that he's no match for me.

ジョギング・サイクリング
jogging, cycling

ジョギング（を）する jog
毎朝5キロくらいジョギングしています。I jog about five kilometers every morning.

ジョギングを始める take up jogging
ジョギングを始めてから、血圧が下がった。My blood pressure has gone down since I started jogging.

ジョギングを続ける continue to jog

サイクリング（を）する take a bike ride
川沿いの道をサイクリングした。I took a bike ride along the river.

サイクリングに行く go for a bike ride

スポーツ
sports

スポーツをする play sports
何かスポーツはしますか？ Do you play any sports?

スポーツが得意［苦手］だ be good [bad] at sports

スポーツ万能だ be an all-around athlete
彼女は頭がよくて、おまけにスポーツ万能だ。She's smart, and she's also good at sports.

相撲
sumo

相撲をとる have a sumo bout

相撲を見に行く go to see sumo
ずっと生で見たかった相撲を、ついに昨日見に行きました。I had wanted to see sumo live for a long time, and I finally went yesterday.

相撲を楽しむ enjoy sumo

ダイエット
diet

ダイエット（を）する go on a diet
メタボ気味なので、ダイエットすることにした。I've decided to go on a diet because I'm a bit overweight.
運動だけでダイエットするのは、難しい。It is hard to lose weight just by exercising.

ダイエット中だ be on a diet
ダイエット中なので、甘い物は一切食べません。I'm on a diet, so I'm not eating sweets.

ダイエットに成功する succeed in dieting
ダイエットに成功して、5キロやせました。My diet has been a success, as I've lost five kilograms.

ダイエットに失敗する fail at dieting

ダイエットに励む try hard to diet

体重
weight

体重を測る weigh oneself

毎日、入浴後に、体重を測っています。I weigh myself every day after taking a bath.

体重が増える gain/put on weight

この2年間で、体重が10キロ増えた。I've gained 10 kilograms in the past two years.

体重が減る lose weight

ウォーキングを始めてから、少し体重が減った。I've lost some weight since I started walking.

体重を落とす／減らす reduce one's weight

テニス
tennis

テニスをする play tennis

週末は友達と、よくテニスをします。I often play tennis with my friends on weekends.

テニスを習う learn tennis

テニスの試合を見る watch a tennis match

テント
tent

テントを張る pitch/put up a tent

私たちは川岸にテントを張った。We pitched our tent on the bank of the river.

テントを片付ける pack up a tent

天気がどんどん悪くなってきたので、大急ぎでテントを片付けた。Since the weather was getting worse and worse, we hurriedly packed up the tent.

テントをたたむ take/pull down a tent

のど
throat

のどが渇く be thirsty; be parched

のどが渇きました。水を1杯もらえませんか？ I'm thirsty. May I have a glass of water?

のどを潤す quench one's thirst

カウンターに座り、冷たいビールでのどを潤した。I sat at the counter and quenched my thirst with a cold beer.

のどが痛む／痛い one's throat aches/hurts

風邪をひいて、のどが痛い。I have a cold and a sore throat.

のどにつかえる／詰まる get something stuck in one's throat

バックパック・リュック
backpack

バックパックを背負う carry a backpack
彼はどこへ行くにも、大きなバックパックを背負っている。He always carries a big backpack around with him.

バックパックに詰め込む pack/stuff ... into a backpack
荷物を全部、バックパックに詰め込んだ。I packed all my stuff into my backpack.

バックパックで旅行する travel with a backpack

花見
cherry-blossom viewing

花見をする enjoy looking at cherry blossoms
会社の同僚と、上野公園で花見をした。I had a cherry-blossom viewing party with my fellow employees in Ueno Park.

花見の場所を取る reserve a spot for cherry-blossom viewing
花見の場所を取るために、彼は朝7時に公園に行った。He went to the park at seven in the morning in order to get a good spot for a cherry-blossom viewing party.

花見に繰り出す go out to see cherry blossoms
花見で騒ぐ have a party under cherry blossoms

虫
insect, worm

虫に刺される be bitten/stung by an insect
虫に刺されて、左腕が腫れ上がった。I was bitten by an insect and my left arm swelled up.

虫がわく be infested with worms
虫を捕る catch an insect
虫を採る／採集する collect insects
虫を除ける repel insects
インディゴには、虫を除ける成分が含まれているそうだ。I hear that indigo contains a component that repels insects.

虫を（殺虫剤で）殺す kill insects (with insecticide)
虫を（虫かごで）飼う keep insects (in a cage)
虫が鳴く an insect chirps

野球（やきゅう）・サッカー **baseball, soccer**	野球（やきゅう）をする play baseball 野球（やきゅう）を見（み）に行（い）く go to a baseball game 　今度（こんど）の週末（しゅうまつ）、野球（やきゅう）でも見（み）に行（い）きませんか？ Would you like to go to a baseball game this weekend? 野球（やきゅう）を観戦（かんせん）する watch a baseball game 　野球（やきゅう）を観戦（かんせん）するのは好（す）きですが、自分（じぶん）ではやりません。 I like watching baseball games, but I don't play myself.

Parties

お祝（いわ）い **celebration**	お祝（いわ）いをする celebrate 　私（わたし）たちは昨日（きのう）、友人（ゆうじん）のマリコの誕生日（たんじょうび）のお祝（いわ）いをした。 Yesterday we celebrated our friend Mariko's birthday. お祝（いわ）いを言（い）う congratulate 　私（わたし）は彼（かれ）に結婚（けっこん）のお祝（いわ）いを言（い）った。 I congratulated him on his marriage. お祝（いわ）いを渡（わた）す give someone a gift/present お祝（いわ）いをもらう receive a gift/present お祝（いわ）いに…をあげる give someone ... as a gift/present 　卒業（そつぎょう）のお祝（いわ）いに、彼女（かのじょ）にバッグをあげた。 I gave her a bag as a graduation gift.
カード **card**	カードを送（おく）る send someone a card 　最近（さいきん）は、メールでクリスマスカードを送（おく）る人（ひと）が多（おお）い。 These days many people send Christmas cards by e-mail. カードを書（か）く write a card カードを受（う）け取（と）る receive a card カードを添（そ）える attach a card 　「誕生日（たんじょうび）おめでとう」というカードを添（そ）えて、彼女（かのじょ）にバラの花束（はなたば）を贈（おく）った。 I gave her a bouquet of roses with a card that said "Happy Birthday."

ごちそう
feast

ごちそうを作る　make/prepare a big meal

パーティーのごちそうを作るので、今朝から忙しい。

I've been busy since this morning preparing a big meal for the party.

ごちそうを用意する　prepare a big meal

ごちそうが並ぶ　there is a big meal

テーブルには、ごちそうがたくさん並んでいた。

There was a lot of wonderful food on the table.

ごちそうを食べる　eat a (big) meal

ごちそうをふるまう　treat someone to a (big) meal

ごちそうする　invite someone for dinner, etc.; treat

今夜の夕食は、僕がごちそうするよ。Tonight's dinner is on me.

ごちそうになる　be treated to dinner; be invited to dinner, etc.

ヨウコに手作りのケーキをごちそうになった。Yoko gave me her homemade cake.

ごちそうを頂く　have/eat a big meal (prepared by someone else)

酒
alcohol, drink

酒を飲む　drink alcohol

酒を飲み過ぎる　drink too much alcohol

パーティーで酒を飲み過ぎて、今朝は二日酔いだ。

I drank too much at the party and am hung over this morning.

酒を買いに行く　go to buy some alcohol

酒を注ぐ　pour (alcoholic) drinks

私はテーブルの全員に、酒を注いだ。I poured sake for everyone at the table.

酒を注いで回る　pour (alcoholic) drinks for others around the table/room

酒を注ぎ足す　add some (more) drink

酒を勧める　offer someone a drink

酒を勧められると、断れない。I can't say no when someone offers me a drink.

酒を一気飲みする　drink ... in one gulp; chug

招待・招待状
invitation

招待する invite
高橋さん夫婦を夕食に招待した。 I invited Mr. and Mrs. Takahashi to dinner.

招待を受ける be invited; accept an invitation
友人の結婚式に招待を受けた。 I was invited to my friend's wedding.

招待を断る decline an invitation

招待状を出す send an invitation

招待状をもらう receive an invitation

たばこ
tobacco,
cigarette

たばこを吸う／のむ smoke
外に行って、たばこを吸ってくるよ。 I'm going outside for a smoke.

たばこを吸い過ぎる smoke too much

たばこを立て続けに吸う chain-smoke cigarettes

たばこをやめる give up/quit smoking
何度もたばこをやめようとしたのだが、結局うまくいかない。 I've tried many times to give up smoking, but I've never succeeded.

たばこを勧める offer someone a cigarette

たばこが嫌いだ hate cigarettes
たばこは嫌いです。たばこを吸う人は、絶対彼氏にしません。 I hate cigarettes. I'd definitely not want a boyfriend who smokes.

たばこは(周りに)迷惑だ cigarette smoke is annoying (to others)

たばこの火を借りる ask someone to give one a light

たばこに火をつける light (up) a cigarette

たばこの火を消す extinguish/put out a cigarette

たばこ(の火)をもみ消す stub out a cigarette

たばこの灰が落ちる cigarette ashes fall

誕生日
birthday

誕生日である be one's/someone's birthday
今日が妻の誕生日だってことを、すっかり忘れていた。 I totally forgot it was my wife's birthday today.

誕生日を迎える celebrate one's birthday
祖母は今年、８０歳の誕生日を迎える。 My grand-

233

mother will celebrate her 80th birthday this year.

誕生日を祝う celebrate someone's birthday

高級レストランで食事をして、彼女の誕生日を祝った。We celebrated her birthday with dinner at a fancy restaurant.

誕生日を忘れる forget one's/someone's birthday

パーティー
party

パーティーをする have/give/throw a party

土曜日の夜に、クリスマスパーティーをします。We're having a Christmas party on Saturday night.

パーティーを開く have/give/throw a party

パーティーに呼ぶ invite someone to a party

パーティーに呼ばれているのですが、何を着ていけばいいのかわかりません。I've been invited to a party, but I don't know what to wear.

パーティーに招待する invite someone to a party

パーティーに行く go to a party

パーティーに行きたかったのだけれど、仕事で行けなかった。I wanted to go to the party, but I couldn't because I had to work.

パーティーに出席する attend a party

プレゼント・
贈り物
gift, present

プレゼントを選ぶ choose a gift/present

母の日のプレゼントを選びに、デパートへ行った。I went to the department store to choose a Mother's Day gift.

プレゼントを買う buy a gift/present

家族にクリスマスプレゼントを買うために、貯金しています。I'm saving to buy my family Christmas gifts.

プレゼントを渡す hand someone a gift/present

プレゼントをあげる give someone a gift/present

彼女に結婚祝いのプレゼントをあげたいのですが、何がいいでしょうか？ I want to give her a wedding gift. What would be good?

プレゼントを贈る give someone a gift/present

プレゼントを受け取る accept a gift/present

プレゼントをもらう get/receive a gift/present

男の子は、両手で抱えきれないほどのプレゼントをもらって、ご満悦だった。The boy looked very happy to receive more presents than he could hold in his arms.

プレゼントを開ける open a gift/present

私はわくわくしながら、プレゼントを開けた。I was excited to open the gift.

プレゼントを気に入る like a gift/present

プレゼントを気に入ってもらえるとうれしいです。I hope you like my gift.

プレゼントを交換する exchange gifts/presents

話題
topic, subject

話題になる be the center of attention; be much talked about

話題を変える change the topic/subject

話題が移る the topic/subject turns to ...

話題は最近見た映画に移った。The conversation turned to the movies we watched recently.

話題が飛ぶ the topic/subject jumps

彼の話は次々に話題が飛ぶので、ついていくのが大変だ。He jumps from one topic to another, so it's hard to keep up.

話題が豊富だ can speak on a variety of topics

彼女は話題が豊富なので、話していて飽きることがない。I never get bored talking with her because she can speak on a variety of topics.

話題にする talk about

Fashion

おしゃれ
fashion

おしゃれ(を)する dress up

珍しく彼がおしゃれをして、パーティーにやってきた。He came to the party all dressed up, which is unusual.

おしゃれに興味がある be interested in clothes

この年代の女の子は誰でも、おしゃれに興味があっ

て当たり前だ。It's natural that girls this age should be interested in fashion.

おしゃれを楽しむ enjoy dressing up

おしゃれにこだわる be particular about what one wears

彼はああ見えて、実は結構おしゃれにこだわっている。It doesn't look like it, but he is rather particular about what he wears.

おしゃれにむとんちゃくだ not care about what one wears

姉はモデル並みに美人なのに、おしゃれにはむとんちゃくだ。My sister is really good-looking like a fashion model, but doesn't care about what she wears.

おしゃれにお金をかける spend a lot on clothes

20代のころは、かなりおしゃれにお金をかけたものです。I used to spend a lot on clothes during my twenties.

サングラス sunglasses

サングラスをかける put on one's sunglasses

おしゃれのためだけでなく、強い日差しから目を守るためにも、サングラスをかけたほうがいい。You should wear sunglasses, not just for fashion but to protect your eyes from strong sunshine.

サングラスをする put on one's sunglasses

サングラスをとる take off one's sunglasses

その歌手はサングラスをとると、まるで別人のように印象が変わる。That singer looks totally different without his sunglasses.

サングラスが似合う sunglasses suit someone

サンダル sandals

サンダルを履く put on one's sandals

サンダルを履いていたせいか、その高級レストランに入店を断られた。I was not allowed to enter the fancy restaurant, maybe because I had my sandals on.

サンダルをつっかける slip on one's sandals

(新しい)サンダルを下ろす wear one's new sandals

サンダルに履き替える change to sandals
　ビーチに着いてすぐ、サンダルに履き替えた。We changed to sandals as soon as we got to the beach.

スーツ
suit

スーツを新調する buy a new suit
　その会でスピーチをするよう頼まれ、スーツを新調した。I was asked to make a speech at the party, so I bought a new suit.

スーツを着こなす dress well in a suit
　上司はいつも、高級スーツをぱりっと着こなしている。My boss is always well dressed in expensive suits.

スーツを仕立てる／オーダーする have a suit tailored

スーツで決める look sharp in a suit

デパート・
ブティック
department store,
boutique

デパートに行く go to a department store
　妻と娘は元日早々、朝早く家を出てデパートに行った。My wife and daughter left for the department store early in the morning on New Year's Day.

デパートで買い物をする shop at a department store

デパートで…を買う buy ... at a department store
　渋谷のデパートで、彼らへの手土産を買った。I bought a present for them at a department store in Shibuya.

デパートで…を選ぶ choose ... at a department store

バーゲン(セール)
(bargain) sale

バーゲンで…を買う buy ... on sale; buy ... in a sale

バーゲンで散財する spend a lot of money at a sale
　そんなつもりはなかったのに、ついついバーゲンで散財してしまった。I spent a lot of money at a sale, though I didn't intend to.

バーゲンでまとめ買いをする buy something in bulk at a sale
　タオルや靴下などの雑貨は、いつもバーゲンでまとめ買いをしています。I usually buy things like towels and socks in bulk at sales.

バーゲンに(人が)殺到する rush into a sale

ブーツ
boots

ブーツを履く put on one's boots
　最近は、夏でもブーツを履いている人を見かける。Recently, I see people wearing boots even in summer.

ブーツを脱ぐ take off one's boots

ブーツを合わせる wear/choose boots to match one's outfit

彼女はミニスカートに、ひざまでのブーツを合わせた。 She chose knee-high boots to go with the miniskirt.

ブーツを修理する repair one's boots

水着
bathing suit

水着を着る put on one's bathing suit

水着になる change into one's bathing suit; be in one's bathing suit

ここのところかなり太ってきたので、水着にはなりたくない。 I don't want to be in my bathing suit as I've gained quite a lot of weight recently.

水着に着替える change into one's bathing suit

彼女はホテルに着くとすぐ、水着に着替えてプールに直行した。 As soon as she got to the hotel, she changed into her bathing suit and went straight to the swimming pool.

水着を買う buy a bathing suit

水着を買い替える buy a new bathing suit (to replace an old one)

Other Hobbies & Interests

アニメ
anime

アニメを制作する produce anime

どこでもいいから、アニメを制作している会社に就職したい。 I'd like to get employed by any company that produces anime.

アニメを見る watch anime

日本のアニメを見て、日本に興味を持ちました。 Watching Japanese anime made me interested in Japan.

アニメになる be made into anime

アニメ化される be made into anime

アニメのコスプレをする get dressed up as one's favorite anime character

会場はアニメのコスプレをした人で、いっぱいだった。The venue was full of people dressed up as their favorite anime characters.

アニメがドラマ化される anime is made into a drama

アニメが映画化される anime is made into a movie; produce a movie version of an anime

木
tree

木を植える plant a tree

いくつかの企業が、環境のために木を植える運動を行っている。Some companies are carrying out tree-planting activities for the environment.

木を切る／切り倒す cut down a tree

木の枝を払う／ 切る cut a branch off a tree; chop a branch off a tree

木に登る climb a tree

子猫は他の猫に追いかけられて、その木に登った。The kitten was chased by some other cat and climbed up the tree.

木が生い茂る trees grow thickly

にぎやかな街の中心から２０分ほど歩いただけで、木が生い茂る森に着いた。Just a 20-minute walk from the busy city center brought us to a forest lush with trees.

木が倒れる a tree falls down

昨日の台風で、道路脇の木が数本倒れた。A few trees fell down on the side of the street during yesterday's typhoon.

木が枯れる a tree dies

木を枯らす kill a tree

木を植え替える transplant a tree

ギャンブル・競馬
gambling,
horseracing

ギャンブルをする gamble

彼は時々、ギャンブルをしに、ラスベガスへ行く。He sometimes goes gambling in Las Vegas.

ギャンブルで身を持ち崩す ruin oneself by gambling

ギャンブルで勝つ［負ける］win [lose] in gambling

ギャンブルで儲ける win money in gambling

彼はギャンブルで儲けた金を、困っている人に匿名で寄付した。He anonymously donated money won from gambling to people in need.

ギャンブルで借金をする go into debt from gambling

クラブ
club

クラブに行く go to a club

クラブに繰り出す go out to a club

みんなで六本木のクラブに繰り出した。We all went out to a club in Roppongi.

クラブで踊る dance at a club

クラブで踊り明かして、朝帰りした。I came home in the early morning after dancing all night at the club.

クラブでナンパする be on the prowl at a club

クラブに入り浸る hang out in a club

ゲーム
game

ゲーム（を）する play a game

ゲームがはやる a game becomes popular

近頃は、知識を身につけられるゲームがはやっている。Games in which players can acquire some knowledge are popular these days.

ゲームを広める make a game popular

ゲームのルールを守る observe the rules of a game

ゲームにはまる be hooked on games

趣味
hobby, taste

趣味を持つ have a hobby

仕事にばかりかまけていないで、何か趣味を持つべきだ。You should not only be occupied with your work but also have a hobby.

趣味が多い have various hobbies

趣味が広い have a wide range of interests

趣味の域を超えている something is more than a hobby

彼の料理は、趣味の域を超えている。His cooking is more than just a hobby.

趣味がない have no particular interest/pastime

趣味がいい［悪い］have good [bad] taste (in ...)

彼女は洋服の趣味がいいので、たまに私の服をコー

ディネートしてもらう。Since she has good taste in clothes, I sometimes ask her to coordinate my outfit.

趣味が高じる one's hobby turns into a profession

彼は趣味が高じて、蕎麦屋を始めてしまった。He turned his interest in soba into a profession and opened his own restaurant.

**植物・
観葉植物・
植木・花
plant, flower**

植物を育てる grow plants

植物に水をやる water plants

私が留守の間、ベランダの植物に水をやるのを忘れないでね。Don't forget to water the plants on the balcony while I'm away.

植物を置く have a (potted) plant

その占い師によると、居間の北側に植物を置くと、運気が上がるそうだ。The fortune-teller says that you can improve your luck by setting a plant in the north side of the living room.

植物を枯らす let a plant wither (by neglect or inappropriate treatment, etc.)

今まで何度か挑戦したものの、結局毎回植物を枯らしてしまう。I've tried growing plants several times before, but they all ended up dying.

花を咲かせる make a flower bloom

花がしおれる／枯れる a flower withers/dies

花を摘む pick flowers

花を花瓶に挿す put flowers in a vase

花を生ける arrange flowers; put flowers in a vase

**宝くじ
lottery**

宝くじを買う buy a lottery ticket

年末にはいつも宝くじを買うのだが、今年は買いそびれてしまった。I usually buy some lottery tickets at the end of the year, but I failed to do so this year.

宝くじに当たる win a lottery

彼はそのニュースを聞いて、宝くじにでも当たったかのように大喜びした。He shouted for joy at the news, as if he had won a lottery or something.

宝くじが外れる do not win a lottery

パチンコ **pachinko**	パチンコをする play pachinko
	パチンコで勝つ［負ける］win [lose] money playing pachinko
	昨日パチンコで勝ったから、今日のお昼はおごるよ。I won money playing pachinko yesterday, so today I'll treat you to lunch.
	パチンコで摩る lose money playing pachinko
	パチンコで稼ぐ win money playing pachinko
	驚いたことに、パチンコで生活費を稼ぐ人たちが結構いるらしい。To my surprise, a fair number of people play pachinko for a living.
フリーマーケット・ 露店・夜店 **flea market, stall (at a night fair)**	フリーマーケットをのぞく drop by a flea market
	フリーマーケットに出す sell ... at a flea market
	比較的状態のいい洋服を、フリーマーケットに出すことにした。I decided to sell some clothes that were in relatively good condition at a flea market.
	フリーマーケットで買う buy ... at a flea market
	このテーブルは、フリーマーケットで安く買いました。I got this table cheap at a flea market.
	フリーマーケットに出店する set up a booth at a flea market
	露店を冷やかす browse street stands
	夜店が出る there are stalls at the night fair
ペット・猫・犬 **pet, cat, dog**	ペットを飼う have a pet; have/keep ... as a pet
	このマンションでは、ペットを飼ってはいけないことになっている。Pets are not allowed in this apartment.
	猫を拾う find a (stray) cat
	妹は学校帰りによく、猫を拾って家に連れて帰ってきた。My sister would often find cats on her way back from school and bring them home.
	猫をなでる pet one's cat
	猫をかわいがる love one's cat
マッサージ **massage**	マッサージをする massage
	バリ島のホテルで全身マッサージをしてもらって、

本当に気持ちよかった。I had my whole body massaged at a hotel in Bali, and it was really relaxing.

マッサージを受ける get a massage; have ... massaged

マッサージを施す give a massage

漫画
manga

漫画を読む read comics

漫画にはまる become immersed in manga

今、ワインをテーマにした漫画にはまっています。

Now I'm a big fan of a comic about wine.

漫画を描く draw cartoons

漫画がアニメ化される a manga is made into an anime

大好きな漫画がアニメ化されると聞いて、とても楽

しみだ。I hear my favorite manga will be made into

an anime, so I'm really looking forward to it.

漫画がテレビドラマになる a manga is made into a TV

drama

APPENDIX

The following charts show correct, incorrect, and questionable collocations. A ● means the collocation is common or acceptable, a blank means that it is uncommon or unacceptable, and a △ means that it is sometimes said but does not sound correct.

Cooking Methods

	野菜 vegetables	卵 egg	肉 meat	魚 fish
切る cut	●		●	●
さばく ★ dress				●
下ごしらえをする prepare	●		●	●
下味をつける season (beforehand)	●	●	●	●
焼く cook, grill, bake	●	●	●	●
煮る simmer	●		△	●
煮込む stew	●		●	●
炒める fry, stir-fry	●		●	
ソテーする sauté	●		●	●
ゆでる boil	●	●	●	
蒸す steam	●	△	●	●
揚げる deep-fry	●		●	●

dress	●			●	●
ふかす ** steam	●				
<ruby>天<rt>てん</rt></ruby>ぷらにする make into tempura	●			△	●

*   Can also be used of chickens <ruby>鶏<rt>とり</rt></ruby>.

** Can only be used of potatoes じゃがいも, sweet potatoes さつまいも, etc.

Money Matters

	<ruby>高<rt>たか</rt></ruby>い high	<ruby>低<rt>ひく</rt></ruby>い low	<ruby>安<rt>やす</rt></ruby>い cheap	<ruby>多<rt>おお</rt></ruby>い many	<ruby>少<rt>すく</rt></ruby>ない few
<ruby>値段<rt>ね だん</rt></ruby>が the price is . . .	●		●		
<ruby>給料<rt>きゅうりょう</rt></ruby>が the salary is . . .	●	●	●	●	●
<ruby>売<rt>う</rt></ruby>り<ruby>上<rt>あ</rt></ruby>げが sales are . . .				●	●
<ruby>物価<rt>ぶっ か</rt></ruby>が prices are . . .	●	●	●		
ドル・<ruby>円<rt>えん</rt></ruby>が the dollar/yen is . . .	●		●		

Size, Volume, Degree

	<ruby>高<rt>たか</rt></ruby>い tall, high	<ruby>低<rt>ひく</rt></ruby>い short, low	<ruby>大<rt>おお</rt></ruby>きい big	<ruby>小<rt>ちい</rt></ruby>さい small
<ruby>背<rt>せ</rt></ruby>が ★ one's height is . . .	●	●	△	△
<ruby>体<rt>からだ</rt></ruby>が one's body is . . .			●	●
<ruby>木<rt>き</rt></ruby>が the tree is . . .	●	●		
<ruby>山<rt>やま</rt></ruby>が the mountain is	●	●	△	△
<ruby>建物<rt>たてもの</rt></ruby>・ビルが the building is . . .	●	●	●	●
<ruby>割合<rt>わりあい</rt></ruby>が the ratio is . . .	●	●	●	●
<ruby>音<rt>おと</rt></ruby>・<ruby>声<rt>こえ</rt></ruby>が the sound/one's voice is . . .	●	●	●	●
<ruby>気温<rt>きおん</rt></ruby>が the temperature is . . .	●	●		

★　<ruby>背<rt>せ</rt></ruby>が<ruby>高<rt>たか</rt></ruby>い [<ruby>低<rt>ひく</rt></ruby>い] someone is tall [short]

Size, Breadth

	大きい (おお) big	小さい (ちい) small	広い (ひろ) spacious	狭い (せま) narrow, cramped	細い (ほそ) narrow
家が (いえ) the house is . . .	●	●	●	●	
庭が (にわ) the garden is . . .	●	●	●	●	
部屋が (へ や) the room is . . .	●	●	●	●	
道が (みち) the path/road is . . .	△	△	●	●	●
通りが (とお) the road is . . .	△	△	●	●	
川が (かわ) the river is . . .	●	●			●
川幅が (かわはば) the river width is . . .			●	●	
箱が (はこ) the box is . . .	●	●			
目が (め) one's eyes are . . .	●	●			●

Population

	<ruby>大<rt>おお</rt></ruby>きい large	<ruby>小<rt>ちい</rt></ruby>さい small	<ruby>多<rt>おお</rt></ruby>い many	<ruby>少<rt>すく</rt></ruby>ない few
<ruby>人口<rt>じんこう</rt></ruby>が the population is . . .			●	●

Speed

	<ruby>高<rt>たか</rt></ruby>い high	<ruby>低<rt>ひく</rt></ruby>い low	<ruby>速<rt>はや</rt></ruby>い fast	<ruby>遅<rt>おそ</rt></ruby>い slow
<ruby>速度<rt>そくど</rt></ruby>が the speed is . . .			●	●

Learning

	<ruby>習<rt>なら</rt></ruby>う learn	<ruby>学<rt>まな</rt></ruby>ぶ learn	<ruby>練習<rt>れんしゅう</rt></ruby>する practice	<ruby>勉強<rt>べんきょう</rt></ruby>する study
<ruby>日本語<rt>にほんご</rt></ruby>を Japanese	●	●	●	●
<ruby>物理<rt>ぶつり</rt></ruby>を physics		●		●
ピアノを piano	●		●	
ダンスを dance	●		●	

Catching

	とる take, get	つかむ grab, catch	つかまえる catch	とらえる catch
ボールを a ball	●	●		
チャンスを an opportunity		●		
犯人を a criminal			●	●
獲物を game	●		●	●

Destroying

	こわす break, destroy	割る break, smash	くだく smash, pulverize	つぶす crush, squash
花びんを a vase	●	●		
ビルを a building	●			
機械を a machine	●			
岩を a rock		△	●	
窓ガラスを a window		●		

<ruby>皿<rt>さら</rt></ruby>を a plate	●	●		
<ruby>氷<rt>こおり</rt></ruby>を ice		●	●	
お<ruby>金<rt>かね</rt></ruby>を money	△			
<ruby>希望<rt>きぼう</rt></ruby>を hope(s)			●	△
チャンスを an opportunity				●
<ruby>夢<rt>ゆめ</rt></ruby>を a dream	●			●
<ruby>会社<rt>かいしゃ</rt></ruby>を a company				●

Severity

	きびしい severe, strict	きつい tough	つらい painful	こわい frightening
<ruby>顔<rt>かお</rt></ruby> face	●	●		●
<ruby>仕事<rt>しごと</rt></ruby> job	△	●	●	
<ruby>人<rt>ひと</rt></ruby> person	●			●
<ruby>練習<rt>れんしゅう</rt></ruby> practice	●	●	●	

（英文版）日本語 言葉のコンビネーション・ハンドブック
Common Japanese Collocations

2010 年 4 月 26 日　第 1 刷発行

監　　修　　庄司香久子

編　　者　　講談社インターナショナル株式会社

編集協力　　日本アイアール株式会社

発 行 者　　廣田浩二

発 行 所　　講談社インターナショナル株式会社
　　　　　　〒112-8652　東京都文京区音羽 1-17-14
　　　　　　電話　03-3944-6493（編集部）
　　　　　　　　　 03-3944-6492（マーケティング部・業務部）
　　　　　　ホームページ　www.kodansha-intl.com

印刷・製本所　　大日本印刷株式会社

落丁本、乱丁本は購入書店名を明記のうえ、講談社インターナショナル業務部宛にお送りください。送料小社負担にてお取替えいたします。なお、この本についてのお問い合わせは、編集部宛にお願いいたします。本書の無断複写（コピー）は著作権法上での例外を除き、禁じられています。

定価はカバーに表示してあります。